My Story
My Testimony
My Deliverance

Rosalind Woodfox

My Story, My Testimony, My Deliverance

Table of Contents

Special Thanks

This book was not easy to deliver but I thank God for all the mid-wives who were there through-out this process and helped me birth this baby! You know who you are and I LOVE U ALL! Thank you Kateri McKinght for the guidance! Thank you Pastor Barriere! Since the day I met you, every interaction has always been truthful, inspiring, and encouraging. Thank you for taking me under your wing and pushing me to fly!

To the most wonderful children anyone could ever hope for! I LOVE every one of you so dearly. Thank you for giving me the space and time to write. Thank you for the encouragement each one of you gave to me when I shared the contents of the book. The love you gave me was just what I needed. I would never say or do anything to hurt or embarrass you. I will always make you proud. Thank you for helping me reach somebody!

Finally, to my covering, my husband, Dwayne. I honor you, Man of God! I know you didn't fully understand why I had to write this book, but you never questioned me. You gave me 1000% support because of your obedience to God. Thank you for doing something no other man was able to do and that was love, appreciate and treasure Rosalind. Thank you for not taking me for granted or taking advantage of me. Thank you for your patience towards me. Thank you for the shoulder I needed to cry on. Thank you for the laughs just at the right time.

I love you Bae,
Always & Forever!

FOREWORD

Rosalind Woodfox is a devoted wife, a committed mother of 4 wonderful children, and a hardworking employee with character and integrity second to none. I've watched her faith grow from "oh ye of little faith," to "mountain moving faith." There's nothing she won't try. She's as bold as a lion, tough as a hammer and vocal as a trumpet. Knowing all of this about her I sometimes wondered where it all came from and this book helps illuminate the path that has brought us this mighty woman of God.

After Pastoring Elder Rosalind Woodfox for 23 years and hearing her preach, teach, counsel and work in ministry, I thought I had seen everything, but my spiritual daughter has amazed me with this book and I know you will be also. Her Story is extreme! Her Testimony is heart wrenching and her deliverance miraculous! I couldn't put it down until I finished it and you won't be able to put it down either!

This book is a must read for every teenager who's trying to find their way and every adult who's lost their way. Take this journey with Rosalind and you won't lean to your own understanding, but you will trust God more easily and you will see how all things work together for good in your life.

Antoine M. Barriere,
Pastor Household of Faith Family Worship Church Int.

\

PERSONAL REVIEW

I must admit that I initially had a difficult time reading this book. You must understand that I love my wife so much that even though all the hurt and heartbreak she went thru was way before we knew one another. It still caused me to feel angry and upset at how someone could do this to such a wonderful person; but, God helped me to not only finish reading, but to also be a part of the healing process as well.

This is a great book. It honestly deals with what a lot of young women have gone through and are going through now. It also deals with young men- how we were taught to use women as sex toys and then throw them to the side for the next one. Finally, it shows us how God can come into your life, turn it around, heal your hurts, turn that test into a testimony, and help others to heal. This book shows how God will give you a new life despite what the devil thought he destroyed.

I am so proud of my wife for being willing to tell her story. To allow God to speak through her so that others can experience the same healing and breakthrough as she has is so powerful. To help someone to understand that your past does not define you, but it develops you into who you are now in Christ is encouraging. To overcome all the fiery darts of the enemy and come out smelling like a rose is nothing short of miraculous!

- BY DWAYNE C. WOODFOX, SR

Introduction

Like most girls growing up, I always wanted to be a princess. I looked forward to the day my knight in shining armor would come and sweep me off my feet and we would live happily ever after. I wanted to be love and accepted, but at the same time felt that I was not supposed to be accepted because I was different. No matter how hard I tried to be liked by my peers at school, within my family, even at church, I always felt different. I don't have wonderful stories of my childhood. I can't tell you about my great family traditions, the exciting vacations nor the fun summertime memories of my childhood. Don't get me wrong, I was not in an abusive environment. I was blessed to have both parents in the home. I had an older brother and a younger sister. Perhaps I had what they called the "middle child" syndrome, because I did find myself feeling "forgotten about" at times, which probably led to me feeling like it was important to be in the "in crowd." But overall, my surroundings were great. Like I mentioned, I had both mom and dad. That was huge among my friends to have both mom and dad - my real biological dad - in the house living, eating, sleeping, and taking care of his family.

We did not live in a mansion, nor did we have a lot of money. I never experienced being without food, clothes, or shoes. We never had our lights turned off or have been evicted. As a matter of fact, my parents were buying the home we were in and my dad had his own business. For a child today, this seems good but there was one thing that I lacked growing up - feeling love and understanding how to love and be loved. My family did not express themselves emotionally. We never hugged each other and we DEFINTELY did not say "I love you." I remember showing more love to my aunts and uncles at church or our reunions more than I did to my own mom and dad. We seemed very distant from each other.

What was wrong with me? Why did I have this constant desire to feel loved and accepted? Why did I see an ugly duckling whenever I looked in the mirror? Why did I try so hard to "fit" in? Now that I am older and matured in God, I realize, it was just the enemy putting thoughts in my mind that I was not accepted, being looked down upon, and not being truly loved. I went through periods in my life of low self-esteem, depression, and suicidal thoughts. I let men use me repeatedly. And when I got tired of the abuse, I began to use them to satisfy my needs. It was all about love and wanting someone to love me for me. For God so loved the world that He gave His only begotten Son just for me. Love is and has been present all my life. Just as God has plans for all of us (Jer.

29:11), and the enemy is seeking to destroy us, our future and eventually kill our seed (John 10:10a). My assignment is to expose the enemy. The enemy of peer pressure, low self-esteem, depression, and rejection. I don't want to see another young lady or young man experience what I went through. I am truly blessed that I am alive and well to share my story with anyone who will listen. I have learned that some of the things we go through in life is not for us. The majority of things we go through is for somebody else – thanks Pastor!

This book includes accounts of real-life experiences. My story Is my story, there is no changing the facts! I don't mean to offend anyone. If this book stops and make one young lady say "I am worth the wait," then all the pain has been worth it! If it makes a young man say "I am going to respect women," then all the pain has been worth it! If some parent decides to be more open and talk to their son or daughter, then all the pain has been worth it! I had to stop asking God why me and realize that God was saying why not you.

The 1st Time

My parents were very strict on me.   Though, my parents will probably never admit it, I grew up in a household that believed that boys should be boys and girls should be perfect angels.

"Cat, keep your panties up and your dress down!" My mom would always say to me growing up.   I was teased by my friends all the time because I could never go to the basketball games or high school dances. I was soon to be known as "Inmate 222" for the numeric address of my prison. If I had to classify myself in school, I probably was a nerd, even though I would get angry if somebody else called me that. I worked part-time at the city zoo, selling burgers, fries and peanuts. This was my weekly outing.   Since I was not allowed to participate in most extra curriculum activities, I focused on my grades, which were very good. However, as a young girl dreaming of finding prince charming, I would wonder who wanted to get with a member of the science club, or even better a band member. What's so embarrassing about being a band member you ask? I'll tell you what… It was an orchestra type symphony band!

I went through my all of high school years without having a boyfriend. I had many secret crushes, but never a secret admirer. Ok, I did have a few secret admirers, but who in the world likes their secret admirer? My secret admirers were always too short or too goofy. For some reason, like most girls, I liked the older guys. At school, I was crazy about the track stars and basketball stars, but my biggest crush was for a much, much older guy. He was a young doctor that lived in my neighborhood. He would ride the local RTA in the mornings to the local hospital. I thought he was all that.

Anyway, through all my high school years, I had never kissed a boy. I often dreamed of how it would be, how he would caress me, and how we would be madly in love. I wanted to talk to somebody or have somebody talk to me about the boys, love, and sex. I wanted somebody to be honest and open with me. I was too scared and nervous to bring up the topic of boys at home. I was not even allowed to say the s-e-x word in my house.

The only image I had of this is what I saw on television or in the songs that I listened to. Don't get me wrong, the television shows were not open at all to sex back then, but it was the implication. I grew up with singers like Michael Jackson and Prince, singing "Do me baby" or "I wanna rock with you." My friends and I even formed a "Princettes" club because we were all crazy about Prince. If I wasn't listening to MJ or Prince, it was the old school songs. Songs that I now listen to with my husband when…well you know. These songs talk about let's get it on or Caught Up in the Rapture of Love. I realize now more than ever that those words were painting a vision or an image on the inside of me that made me very curious. I began wanting to release those feelings that were bubbling on the inside of me.

I would always look at the "cool girls," the real "popular ones" and wanted to be like them. I wanted to wear nice clothes, something that was not in lay-a-way for months and then by the time I got the clothes out of lay-a-way it out was out of style. I wanted to wear shoes that came from somewhere other than Shoe Town or didn't have the word "coasters" written all over it. I wanted to have a boyfriend or least be able to get a boyfriend.

Well now it was my senior year and because my grades were very good, I had met most of my graduation requirements. With the help of some great connections (thanks dad) I was able to get a better job working with the city. It paid great money….well, for a seventeen-year-old, anything above minimum wage was good. I was able to do what every female loves to do…. SHOP AND GET MY HAIR DONE! For today's average teenager, add nails, toes, and cell phone bill. Boy have times changed.

Anyway, I was determined that this senior year was going to be great! Things quickly changed for me at school. It was like overnight I was being noticed by the boys and I liked it…no, I loved it! After I began making regular visits to the hair dresser and changed my wardrobe, I finally moved off the nerd list. How do I know this? Because boys were talking to me other than asking for help with their homework or if they could cheat on the next test. They were good conversations. I knew I finally arrived when that good-looking doctor that would ride the local RTA in the mornings asked for my phone number. We would always say good morning to one another, but after I had an outside change, he began to bring up conversations about my senior year and college. Eventually one day before I got off the bus at school, he gave me his number and asked me to call him every now and then. I told him that I was not allowed to even talk to boys let alone a grown man on the phone. He said he understood and asked if he could have mine instead. I was nervous, but I gave it to him. He said one day he would be able to make the call. When I got off the bus, I screamed!

Not to long after that, Daryl, one of the more popular seniors in my class, asked me for my phone number. I had a big crush on him. He was nice, funny, and had a great sense of humor. He was always making jokes and making others laugh. I did not care that momma said no boys on the phone I was going to find a way to talk to him and I did. Just because I wanted to "fit in," I began disobeying my parents and sneaking to hook up three way calls on the phone just to talk to him.

The more we talked on the phone, the more I fell head over heels for him. I had all these feelings bubbling inside of me that felt uncontrollable, and every time I saw or talked to him, they were exploding. I knew I could never talk to my mom because she would never understand. For a long time, I was angry with my mom because she never talked to me about boys or what some would call the facts of life. I was so green in that area.

I remember on the first day of Junior High, I had an unexpected visitor arrive, that I later found out would visit me every month. I was scared to death because I did not know what was happening. I thought I was dying. I remember sitting in the bathroom on the toilet yelling for my mom. When she came into the bathroom and saw what happened. She was upset! She said, "Rosalind, you would let something like this happen on a day like today?!" I was a bit confused, but later realized momma just did not know how to operate under pressure. A few days later she gave me a book and said, "Read this." I was even more confused and sick to my stomach with all those graphic pictures.

With moments like these, there were certain things that I knew not to ask about. So, I did what every girl does... talk to her "friends." I say that very loosely, because I don't use the word friend the same way anymore. I have learned through the years that a friend is more than somebody you can go shopping with, spend all day at the mall, come back empty handed, and say you had a great time shopping. A friend is somebody who will tell you the hard-core truth even if it hurts you and them. A friend is somebody that will go the extra mile for you, when there is nothing in it for them. A friend is somebody that moves miles away but is still just a phone call away. A friend is somebody that you can cry to and they will understand even if this is the fiftieth time you've cried about the same thing. A friend is someone who celebrates you and displays it openly. Thank you to all my solid friends...you know who you are! Moving on...

Daryl and I began talking on the phone all the time. We would talk at lunch and again after school. From time to time, I had a science club meeting or tutoring after school and many times, I would be sure to let my mom know how important it was for me to be at those "after school meetings." I just did not let her know the school meeting was 30 minutes and the other 30-50 minutes was my meeting with Daryl.

He was on the basketball team and he was pretty good. It was like a dream to be good friends with a basketball player. He had been playing for two years, but unfortunately, I was never allowed to go to the games...remember Inmate 222. My brother who went to the same school could attend the dances, sports events etc., but I could not.

Anyway, it was my senior year and I was determined to have fun. I always had a dream of being a cheerleader. It would be perfect, me a cheerleader and my soon to be boyfriend a basketball player. My best friend and I mustered up enough guts to try-out for the squad. We worked very hard at it and made it. My best friend's mom was very lenient on her and let her drive the car to school. We already knew that this was a sure thing for the game. I wasn't sure if my mom was going to let me go, but I gave it a try anyway. I had to begin asking her one week before the game. I crossed all my T's and dotted my I's and after much persuasion, she agreed. I just thought mom was being cruel and mean. She never wanted me to

17

have any fun. At least that's what I thought. I now know that she was only trying to protect me, but I could not understand it back then. I was so consumed with having fun and doing my own thing, I was willing to be disobedient, disrespectful, and dumb.

After the game, which we won, everybody wanted to celebrate. My best friend and I spent time together with Daryl and his best friend, Kevin. We both knew I had to be at home by a certain time, but I didn't press the issue, neither did they. The first time I could go somewhere, I stayed out late. I knew it was wrong, but I was having a good time. I wanted to let my "friends" know that I wasn't a wallflower. The guys didn't have a curfew and I wanted to hang out with them. When I got home, I had some lame excuse I gave my mom to try and manipulate myself out of a long punishment. It worked. Even though I was not punished by my mom, I was still punishing myself and I didn't even realize it. Sometimes when you are young you think you are exempt from certain things. I found out later that we all live and die by the choices we make. You reap what you sow. For every lie, for every sassy and disobedient remark I made to my mom, were bad seeds I had begun to sow into my own life. I kept making bad choices, but after all, I thought I was exempt from anything happening to me.

Daryl and I began talking on the phone more and more. We had never kissed, never held hands, and never touched each other. I knew he was a great guy. I knew he would never do anything to hurt me. For a brief moment, my mom was working a night shift, which left me and my younger sister home by ourselves. In one of our conversations I mentioned this to Daryl and he asked if he could come over to the house one night. Now it doesn't take a genius to figure out why he wanted to come over to my house. I had a choice. Nobody was twisting my arm. I told him he could come over tomorrow night.

That day at school, him coming over was the topic of our morning, lunch and after school conversations. That night at home, before my mom even left for work, I knew that he was on the way. I acted like everything was fine, but I still felt nervous. All we were going to do was watch television, but on the inside, I was experiencing that same uncontrollable feeling. When he got there, I was a little shocked because he was dressed casually. I still had the same clothes on from school that day. I let that thought quickly pass because he always dressed very nice. We sat down and watched a little tv, but soon he began saying how much he wanted to see my room.

"Where's your room?" he asked.

At first, I acted like I didn't hear him, but he soon repeated himself.

"It's upstairs, why?" I asked, but I already knew the answer.

"Because I want to see it," he replied.

I knew that I should not bring this boy to my room, but it was exciting to know that he was all into me. It was a little flattering to hear him ask. Deep down, I wanted him to see my room.

"It's just a room," I said. "There's nothing special about it. Besides I thought we were watching television?"

I was toying around and playing with his emotions. I already knew that if we went to my room, things might get a little out of control. Again, here was another chance for me to make a better decision, but I was fulfilling my desires. I totally forgot that my sister was in the house. I could be in a world of trouble if my parents found out, but it didn't matter to me. I finally agreed, and we went upstairs to my room.

I was so nervous walking up those steps. I knew that this was wrong, but I didn't have the willpower to stop. After a few minutes of being in my room, he started asking all these questions.

"Can I get a hug?" he asked.

"A hug?" I asked.

"Yeah, just one quick hug, that's all." he explained.

I gave him a hug and thought to myself, is this really happening? Daryl is at my house, in my room! Oh my God!

"Roz, have you ever done it?" he asked.

Umm, done it," I hesitated. "No, I haven't."

"Rosalind, I would love to be your first," he said. "Can I be your first? It won't hurt."

"Daryl, I don't think so." I said.

I told him no, but I was hesitant. I was scared, but at the same time I thought, what am I waiting for? I was sitting on the side of the bed thinking and rationalizing why I shouldn't, and Daryl was sitting next to me telling me all the reasons why I should.

"Roz, you know I like you a lot," he said. "And I thought that you liked me too? I promise that it won't hurt. Please Roz? Please Roz? Pleeeze?"

He was rubbing my back and playing with my hair. It was very distracting but at the same time, I liked it. He probably said please Roz a hundred times. This was somebody that I really liked. I thought about him all the time. Whenever I was around him, I had a feeling that didn't happen when I was around other guys. I was living for that moment so, I decided to lose my virginity that night. We agreed that it would be just between us. Before anything happened, he told me that he was going to use a condom. I was so caught up in the moment that I didn't even think to ask. However, when he mentioned it, I felt relieved because momma would always talk about how getting pregnant was not an option. She would not talk to me about sex, but she would say, "Do not come home pregnant." As a matter of fact, she seemed very uncomfortable when she said the word sex. It always sounded like she was saying sect, instead of sex. That's just how much she didn't like the word. I remember her saying, "you better not get pregnant because if you do, I'm gonna send yo behind to the country." I think she said this in hopes to scare me from ever having sex, since I was such a city girl. We would visit my grandparents who lived in the country and there was nothing there but cotton fields and dirt roads. Anyway, when he said condom, I felt protected.

It was the night that I dreamed about for a long time. Even though this was not quite what I thought it would be like: no soft music playing, and nobody carrying me over the threshold in my wedding dress. No candles were burning and the curtain was not billowing from the night breeze. I really wanted this night to be special. Daryl turned off the lights and then we laid on the floor, the hard floor. I had my eyes closed tightly, as if I was about to get on a roller coaster. I was too scared to say anything, mainly because I didn't want my sister to come upstairs. Within minutes it was all over. It was over so fast that I thought I missed something. Everything I dreamed would happen, never happened. He didn't kiss me, caress me or stroke me. I thought for sure there was supposed to be a kiss involved in your first time. I laid there stunned because it was not special at all. I was in total shock.

"Roz...Roz," he called. "Roz get up and put your panties on." Daryl had to call my name a few times before I snapped out of it.

Instead of feeling like I was on top of the world, I remember feeling dirty, embarrassed, and ashamed. I could barely look him in the face anymore. I felt horrible. He seemed to be fine. He quickly got dressed and then gave me a kiss on the check. He said he had to get home. I walked him out and quickly ran back upstairs. I immediately jumped in the shower and washed and washed. I scrubbed so hard thinking I could get rid of the dirty feeling on my body but those feelings of guilt and shame cannot be washed away by natural water.

Instantly I felt different all over my body, and not in a good way. I was on an emotional rollercoaster. I kept replaying everything over in my mind. No matter what scenario I replayed, it all had the same ending. If I would have just taken more control of my emotions and feelings, none of this would have happened. I had a choice and I made a very bad one. It was not Daryl's fault, it was my fault. I just felt as if I didn't have anything inside of me to help me overcome. I eventually told myself to put the whole thing behind me. I just wanted all those feelings to go away, not to mention all the lies that I had told. I cried myself to sleep and glad this night was over.

I woke up in the morning and nothing had changed. I was feeling worse. Not only was I feeling dirty, embarrassed and ashamed, but I was feeling used. I realized because of my stupid decision, I allowed him to use me for his 5 minutes, excuse me, 2 minutes of pleasure. I had never felt so depressed in my life. I should have tried to fake a sickness, so I would not face him at school in a few short hours. But I was not so fortunate. Instead I had to face him, and even worse was facing all his buddies at school he promised not to tell.

I was walking down the hall immediately after homeroom and I heard somebody call me. I was still in a daze that the person had to call me two or three times.

"Hey Roz...Good Morning.... Hello." somebody called.

It was Daryl! I did not even recognize his voice. When I lifted my head up, I could barely look him in the eyes. But I did see all his buddies looking at me as if they had just gotten the 411 news. I quickly put my head down and rushed to 1st period. I could hear the guys laughing. When I glanced back, I saw them all giving him dap, like he was the man. I went from not having much attention to having all the attention.

Daryl and I never talked like we used to after that day. When he called, I felt so betrayed, that my words were very limited, the conversation lasted less than 10 minutes. A few short weeks later, I found out that he was dating a sophomore, some underclassmen. He was crazy about her. He was carrying her books, opening doors for her and surprising her with cute little stuffed animals. Their relationship lasted through her high school graduation. A few years later I heard through the grapevine that they were getting married. All the feelings I once had for him, ended at once because I thought that was going to be me.

I told my best friend Robyn what happened once I realized that it was over between us. She was excited that I lost my virginity. I wanted her to feel bad like I did. But after listening to her and discovering that she was not a virgin, I didn't feel too bad. She was dating another basketball player and they occasionally played one on one. She was going on and on about how good "it" was. As she was trying to tell me, she was getting all caught up. She started shaking her head, lifting her hands and calling on the Lawd, just like a sister in church with a new shiny rock on her finger.

I thought to myself there must be something that I missed. Since there was nothing I could do about the past, I decided to move on. I had lost my virginity, my self-respect, and self-esteem. I just wanted to put a band-aid on this wound and create a better memory.

Did he tell you?

Since my humiliating experience with Daryl, I was in the habit of hanging around after school. Robyn and her boy would leave in her mom's car, so I was kind of by myself. After school one day, my friend Tasha was waiting on her brother to pick her up and I was standing outside on the steps just staring at the cars. We had known each other since 9th grade. When I first met Tasha, I thought she was younger because she was very immature, and she was always telling jokes. She was always making people laugh or humming a tune as she walked to class. You could always expect a laugh if you were in the same class. I like being around her because she was hilarious. Tasha, like me, didn't have much experience with the boys either. As outgoing as she was when it came to telling jokes, she was comfortable; however, with boys, she was very shy. Tasha was buck-toothed and was very short. I think that had a lot to do with the type of play she was getting from the boys. It seemed like each school year we talked on the phone more and more, this was especially the case since it was our senior year. One day, I was waiting with Tasha on the steps because her brother was picking her up from school. Tasha was so funny because she rode in a car wherever she went. She refused to catch the RTA. She depended on her mom, dad, or brother to give her a ride everywhere. I remember when her brother pulled up because it was a nice black Camry with tinted windows, smooth sound system, and shiny rims. She gathered her things and headed towards the car. I decided to leave as well since it was getting late. I don't even remember getting a glimpse of her brother, but apparently, he saw me. Later that night Tasha called me with the news.

"Hey girl, I got some news for you" she said.

I asked, "what news are you talking about…what happened?"

"Girl, my brother likes you! When we drove off today, he asked me who you were. I told him that was Roz and that we had been friends since 7th grade. He said he wanted to meet you."

I was a little nervous, but at the same time flattered that he was interested. I was still upset about Daryl and was looking for a way to get over him.

"Tasha what should I do?" I became nervous suddenly.

"Girl, I don't know. All I know is that he thinks you're cute and…."

She hesitated like she was about to say something else.

"And what, what were you about to say?"

26

"Nothing, well, it is something…it's a couple of things. First, I just don't want you to get hurt again."

"What do you mean again?" I asked.

"You didn't have to tell me anything about you and Daryl, but I know something has been going on with you. For a while you have been walking around with your head down. Everybody knew that you had a crush on that dude for a while." I also know that you were not out there cheering at the games because you like basketball so much."

Tasha was always right. She always had a way of digging deep into a situation. I thought she was great at observing and analyzing things. In other words, she was nosey. I told her about what happened, and she just told me to keep my head up. But just like Robyn, she was excited too that I wasn't a virgin anymore as well. I really starting thinking this was a good thing. Besides momma said don't get pregnant, so everything should be fine. This is what I kept telling myself, but still something on the inside of me was still ashamed. I still cried in the shower because I wanted to turn back the clock, but it was forever too late. I just decided to cover up my horrible experience and act like everything was okay. This was a secret I just had to hold in for a very long time.

"What's the other thing Tasha?" I asked.

"Girl, this is not my real brother, he's adopted," She said.

I listened carefully, but I couldn't understand why she was telling me that. Well that wasn't everything.

"Roz, he's not that cute, but he is a sweet person."

My Story, My Testimony, My Deliverance

I was very interested in meeting Tasha's brother. It's crazy because I knew he was older than me and he had a nice ride. This was a step up from Daryl. Well, Tasha and I both loved pizzas. I remember one day we decided to ask her brother to come and pick us up and drop us off at a pizza parlor near the school. It was our way of letting me check Benny out. I made sure that I was looking extra good this day. Tasha called and asked her brother to drive us to the pizza parlor and he told her no. However, when she mentioned that I was going, he rearranged his schedule. Benny got there fast and before we got in the car, Tasha told me to play it cool and not to say anything.

"Benny, this is Roz. Roz this is Benny." She said.

"How ya doing?" I did not say anything else. I was so interested in checking him out. He wasn't bad at all. Yes: he was dark skinned: Daryl was high yellow, so it was a nice change. I knew this was not going to be my Prince Charming. I always knew that I would never marry a dark skin man. I remember telling my momma, my husband was going to be light skin with pretty eyes. Tasha and I talked about school, and other stuff. It was weird because Benny wasn't really saying anything to me but he was commenting or agreeing with everything that I said. He dropped us off and asked how we were getting back to school. Both of us said we were going to walk, since it was only 15 minutes away. He looked at his watch and said he had to run a quick errand, but he could pick us up.

"Tasha girl, he is not that bad. I thought the boy was going to be scary looking."

"Well, I know he likes you because he gave me $20 dollars to pay for the pizza. He never gives me any money. I don't care how much I beg. He is trying to impress you."

He came back like he promised and this time he was a lot more talkative. The next couple of days Tasha and I were getting chauffeured around like movie stars. Benny would bring us wherever we wanted to go. Every now and then he would need to run an errand, but he was always there. Benny didn't live with Tasha's family because he was much older. But it seemed like every time we were on the phone, he was always popping in. I could hear him in the background and he would always tell Tasha to tell me hello. Eventually, she would just give him the phone and we would talk for a little while. It was obvious there was some chemistry between us.

Well, we were still in basketball season at school and there was a Friday night game. Since Robyn was still all involved with her "boo," I really didn't want to be a third wheel and tag along with them. It must have been meant to be because Benny volunteered to bring Tasha and I to the next basketball game. Up until that night we had never even held hands, but this night was different. After the game, we got something to eat. Then Benny asked the weirdest question.

"Tasha, you want to drive?"

"Boy what are you talking about? You never let me dri…" she started then had a split-second thought, "If you're serious, ok."

He pulled over in a parking lot somewhere and Tasha got in the driver's seat. He asked me to come in the back seat with him. I knew it was about to get hot. He told Tasha to drive, but she better be careful of what she was doing. At first, we just talked. He told me that he really liked me and enjoyed spending time together after school. I was in my cheerleading outfit so needless to say I was looking rather cute and at the same time, like I was missing some clothes.

"I want to kiss you," he said

I did not know how to respond. As a matter of fact, I don't remember giving him an answer. It felt a little awkward because my friend was in the car and I felt obligated because he had been driving me around, paying for everything, and he was even giving me money. I didn't want him to get mad or angry at me, so I kissed him. It was my first real kiss. It was wonderful! After that kiss, I forgot all about Tasha being in the car. We were all over each other. This went on for at least thirty minutes. I didn't even know where we were or what part of town we were in. Neither did Tasha, because she was excited about driving. He had to make a quick stop at his house before he brought me home, so I used this time to get my hair and clothes back together. Tasha wanted to know if we did it. I told her of course not, but we were very close. We made the switch back to him driving and Tasha and I being in the back seat again before he made the stop at his house. He pulled up and ran inside.

"Roz, are you alright?" Tasha asked.

"Yeah, I'm fine. I can't believe what almost happened." I said.

"I can't either. Did he tell you?" Tasha asked.

"Tell me what?" I inquired.

"Benny is married… His wife and four kids are right inside that house." Tasha stated.

"Tasha, you are lying. Why didn't you tell me?" I exclaimed.

"Because it was none of my business. I told him that he needed to tell you. He was supposed to do it tonight." She said defensively.

"Well he didn't," I responded in total shock.

Benny got back in the car and I was very quiet. He still didn't know I found out his secret. He brought me home and I went straight upstairs and cried. I could not understand why he would do this and not tell me. I am supposed to be swept off my feet by prince charming, but instead I keep coming up short. We continued our back-seat rendezvous for weeks! Benny was a nice guy. Anything I would ask of him, he did it. I was falling for him. Would he leave his wife? That was stupid for me to even think that because I was only 17 years old. Why in the world would he even consider this? He was obviously in it for the thrill and excitement of having a "high school" girl, a very naïve girl. The craziest thing is that I allowed for these back-seat escapades, free food, and money go on for 2 months!

I would even go by his house as Tasha's friend just to see him, and his wife never suspected a thing, but he was nervous as hell. Even though I knew I was wrong because he had a family, I liked the attention I was getting. Also, the feeling that it was secretive was exciting. But what good is love if you can't share with people around you? Something is wrong if it is only expressed at certain times of the day or when certain people are or are not present. I decided I had enough.

Eventually, I stopped excepting his offers to bring me home, or I declined when Tasha asked if I wanted to go get pizza after school. I knew what those offers really meant. So, while I would be at home taking a cold shower, he would be with his wife. There were no words said, just an understanding that this was not meant to be.

I did not feel good about myself once we stopped seeing each other. I continued to put up the wall around me that started after my experience with Daryl. I was not going to let anyone take advantage of me again. It was all about me and having fun.

Toy Soldiers

Free at last, free at last, thank God almighty, I'm free at last! Finally, I made it, 18 years old. I am grown, or at least I thought I was grown. You know in the world we live in today, any 18-year-old associates their age with independence. I later found out that with age comes responsibility and maturity. All I thought in my mind was that I can do whatever I want, I can say whatever I want, but most importantly I can GO where ever I want! That was my attitude. For once and for all, I was going to experience everything life had to offer. As I mentioned earlier, I always made good grades. I went to a college prep school, so college was obviously the next choice, but not the only choice. There were local recruiters from the Army who came to my school and administered the ASVAB test to all graduating seniors. It was a military aptitude exam. I didn't want to take this test because it lasted for at least 2 hours, maybe more. I sat next to my classmate Yolanda, and we both thought taking this test was a waste of time because neither of us ever thought about the military. We both decided to mark anything on the test. It was like a joke to us. This should eliminate us from being considered. I had always dreamed of attending college and having fun. It was going to be the first time I was on my own and experiencing life. I wanted to go to the historically black all female college in Georgia. I had always wanted to go there. I submitted all my paperwork, met all the deadlines, and I was just waiting on my acceptance letter. The day finally came. I got home and saw the letter sitting on the television. It read something like this:

"Dear Applicant,

Thank you for your interest in Spelman College. We have reviewed your application, test scores etc. Unfortunately, at this time, we have accepted all incomings students for the Fall Semester. You have been placed on a waiting list…"

I don't remember reading anything else. I was devastated. All the hard work, all the studying, all the A's & B's? This was not fair. I had been working hard for years. This was not supposed to happen to somebody who was in the top 15% of their graduating class. Where do I go from here? I was so smart that I did not apply to any other school. I put all my eggs in one basket. Perhaps I could quickly apply to some local universities, but I had missed the deadlines to apply for financial aid. This would have put a strain on my family and deep down I did not want to be too close to home.

My Story, My Testimony, My Deliverance

A few days later, I received a strange phone. It was a local recruiter from the United States Army Reserve. Ironically, I received a passing score on the aptitude test and they wanted to talk to me about a future in the military. After all the hard work in school which landed me nowhere, I decided to join the Reserves. This would put some money in my pocket and just give me a break away from all the studying. What was even more ironic is that Yolanda also received a passing score, so she and I enlisted together.

A few days before I left for basic training, I bumped into Johnathan. The doctor from the morning bus.

"Hi Rosalind, it's good to see you." he said. "Are you eighteen yet?" Johnathan would always ask that question ever since we exchanged phone numbers that day. He would always implicate to me that when I turned eighteen, he was going to make a move. I didn't answer the question, I just blushed instead. "Johnathan, you are so funny." I laughed. "How is the new car? I had been seeing you around town in your Benz, so I knew why you weren't catching the bus anymore."

"The car is fine," he said. "But you didn't answer my question. Are you eighteen yet and can I see you before you leave for college?"

"I'm not going to college," I kind of said with disappointment. "Spelman placed me on a waiting list and I can't wait. I need to get away, make some money, and enjoy life."

"So, what are you going to do?" he asked.

"I joined the Reserves and I leave next week!" I announced. "One of my classmates, Yolanda is going with me under the Buddy System. We signed our contracts together and we can't be separated at all!"

"I'm shocked, because you don't look like an Army girl," he said. "You have too much brains for that. I thought you wanted to go to Law School?"

"I know but it will all work out." I said.

"Well, I guess I'll have to take you out after you get back," he said. "I can't wait to see you after you tone up. When do you get back?"

"In about 6 months." I said with hope, trying to convince myself that it was not that long.

"Ok, well you take care." he said as he kissed me on the check and left.

I really didn't know what to expect when I arrived at Boot Camp. But it was no secret that I went from one strict environment to another strict environment. This was not good. I could not say or do what I wanted, not to mention go where I wanted. It was worse than being at home.

The female Privates were always threatened if we were caught fraternizing or talking with a male Private. It was almost like your mom telling you not to get a cookie out of the cookie jar although all of the cookies were hot and fresh from the oven. You know…the homemade kind like grandma used to make. The kind you would slap yo' mamma for. Forgive me, but you know what

I'm talking about. After years of confinement, with 6 weeks extra time, I was ready to cut loose.

Graduation night from Boot Camp was a coming out party. Yolanda and I hit every party on and off base we knew about. There was not a party that didn't have liquor, cigarettes, nor X-rated activities. Nobody was there to tell us anything, except the MP, military police, but luckily, we were never at the scene when they showed up. You could only imagine what most of the graduates were planning. We were around the same sex day in and day out, and now a taste of freedom. But something happened. Both Yolanda's mom and my mom came to our graduation as a surprise. We really were not expecting this. So, we had a plan. Yolanda and I decided to spend the afternoon with our moms graduation day but ditch them that evening. We left around 6pm and did not see them anymore until 6:00am the next morning. We stayed out partying all night long. We made it back to the hotel just in time enough to tell our parents goodbye and make 7:00am curfew back on the base.

I think my mom was disappointed that we didn't spend more time together, but there was nothing she could do about it.

Immediately after graduation, we started AIT, our military training course, which lasted for about two months. Even though we still had responsibilities around the barracks, after class it was our own free time. I kind of felt like I was away at college because I had finally got some freedom. AIT school was like a mini campus. There was a bowling alley, gym, Px (military idea of

Walmart), and even a club (the military calls it a Pub). After school hours, you could go and come as you please, but only if you made curfew. Yolanda and I were always going somewhere after school. Right across from the female barracks were the men barracks. Yolanda and I both were very anxious to meet and greet our neighbors. One day while we were at the Px, I thought I had finally met prince charming. He was tall, light, and handsome, he just didn't have pretty, brown eyes, but what the heck.

"Don't you live in Alpha across the street from us?" he asked

"Yes, I'm Rosalind, and this is Yolanda," I replied. "But you can call me Roz."

He was so good lookin' I was not about to let Yolanda get a chance.

"My name is Eric," he said. "But you can call me Hamp." He preferred to be called by his last name. This was military procedure. He was sold-out for the military. Every time I saw him, he was lookin' sharp. I think Hamp was the reason I fell in love with seeing a man in a uniform. He made it look so good. He had a certain confidence about himself when he walked. We began having lunch and dinner together in the mess hall everyday day.

"So, Hamp, what are your plans after AIT?" I asked and waited eagerly for a response.

"I am going to work at the Pentagon in Special Intelligence," he said boastfully. "What about you?"

"Well, I am going back to New Orleans," I said a little embarrassed. "I was on the waiting list for Spelman before I

38

enlisted. I am going to move on from that dream. I think I am going to apply to a local college for the Spring Semester."

"You know I would love if you would come to Washington and visit me," he said. "I really enjoy being with you. I think we can have a long-distance relationship and see where it takes us."

Did he just ask me to be his G.I. Jane? Part-time lover? Whatever he was asking I was willing to take it anyway that I could get it. I had a very good feeling about Hamp and I was willing to take a chance. I couldn't wait to get back to my room and tell Yolanda about what he said.

"Yo, you not gonna believe this!" I exclaimed. "Hamp said that he wants me to come to Washington after AIT school to visit. He says that we could have a long-distance relationship."

"Do you believe him?" she asked. "You have only been knowing Hamp for 2 months."

"Yolanda, I have been waiting a long time for prince charming and I think Hamp is it." I said. "He wants to spend next weekend with us." I announced.

"What!", shouted Yolanda. "Are you serious?"

"Yes," I said. "You know we both have our free weekend pass and I was hoping that we could all hang out and have some fun."

"Roz, that's fine, just please be careful." Yolanda said.

I could hardly wait until 5:00pm Friday, because this was going to be a great weekend. Free weekends were so cool, because all you had to do was sign out and be back by Sunday night curfew. I already had a bag packed and reservations at a hotel off base. Yolanda, Hamp, myself and a few others all took a cab to the hotel, got changed, and began partying.

I think we were all glad that nobody knew we were soldiers. We were not required to wear our uniform, nor those uncomfortable boots. We were just ordinary people. Hamp and I were inseparable. We were acting like a couple. I was so nervous because I never hung out with a guy before. Remember, I went straight from home, to boot camp, to here. From Daryl, to Benny to here. I knew I was green, but I also knew I needed to experience life. This was a brand-new beginning for me and I wanted to forget the hurts of the past. Hamp was going to be good for me.

We all hung out eating and drinking until about 10'o clock Friday and Saturday. Then we would come back to the hotel and pile up in one room and play cards, drink some more and laugh until the wee hours in the morning. By the time Saturday night rolled around my confidence in kissing had elevated to an all-time high. That's all Hamp and I did was kiss each other. He was fantastic! Around 11 o'clock, Hamp went back to his room. He said he was tired and wanted to get some rest. We gave each other a long passionate kiss and said good night.

I stayed in the room with the others and watched an intense game of Spades. About a half hour later Hamp called the room and ask me to come upstairs to his room. I told Yolanda, I would be right back because it was getting late and we had to check out in the morning. When I got to his room, he was acting a little weird. It was like he wanted to say something, but it wouldn't come out.

"Why did you call me up here?" I asked with a smile.

"I was thinking about you," he said. "I got tired of being down there with all those people."

"Yeah, how many games of spades can anybody play?" I said jokingly. Before I could get the last sentence out, he interrupted me with a question.

"Roz, are you a virgin?" he blurted out.

I really didn't know how to answer this question. I know that Daryl and I had a mini experience, which lasted 5 minutes, but was that the real thing? If I say no, he might look down on me. If I say yes, he might not want to be with me. What do I do?

"Uh, I don't know," I answered with my head down. "I had a quick, quick thing with somebody that I really liked but to be honest with you it wasn't pleasurable. It was so quick that I wonder if I am a virgin or not."

"Roz, I want to be with you right here, right now," he whispered. "I promise I will not hurt you. I know I asked you to come to Washington after AIT, and even though we will be graduating in about three weeks I don't want to wait."

He was so charming, I could not resist the temptation. I was so hot everywhere. All those familiar bubbly feelings were present again. It was the perfect atmosphere. Just he and I with the soft music playing. The gentleness of the sheets and pure passion. Hamp and I spent the night together. By the time Sunday morning came, I knew that I was a virgin no more! I had fallen head over heels with Hamp. Three more weeks until graduation and I was ready to pack up things in New Orleans and move to Washington. Hamp and I spent the last few weekends together, talking about graduation, and the future. He was scheduled to graduate Friday morning, and we were graduating that afternoon. Yolanda and I made our airline reservations to go home 2 months prior. We were scheduled for a late flight out that same night. A few days before graduation, Hamp told me that he was looking forward to celebrating together.

"What time do you graduate on Friday?" he asked.

"3 o' clock," I replied. "I know that you will be leaving that morning, so I will make sure that I call you when I arrive in New Orleans that night."

"I am not leaving out until Saturday morning," he said. "I wanted you and I to spend one last night together."

I told him that Yolanda and I already booked our flight months ago and our parents were expecting us home Friday night. I guess the part about parents expecting us home, didn't sound too adult like.

"Look Roz, here is the name of the hotel I'm staying at," he said. "We can meet up around 7pm."

He was so convincing. I was willing to do whatever I had to just to spend that last night with him. Now, if only I could convince Yolanda. She was not going for it at all. This meant that we needed to call the airport, change the flight and then call our parents and make up some excuse for not coming home tomorrow night. I reminded Yolanda that we were in this together and that she had to stay one extra night with me, so I could hook up with Hamp. I don't know why, but she bought it.

I spent all afternoon and night, calling the airline to make the change and calling around town to book a hotel room. I thought we would never find a room because there were so many AIT school graduations going on that weekend. But luckily everything was working out with the airline and the hotel. Now I just needed to call my mom and make up a lie about why we had to stay one more day. Once my mom bought it, Yolanda called and told her mom the exact same lie.

After everything was settled, I called Hamp at his barracks and gave him the hotel number where we were going to be staying. Hamp and I agreed to get together around 7 o'clock that night, but I was ready at six sharp. I was ready to tell Hamp that I loved him. As soon as he got his assignment in Washington, I was booking my flight. I could not wait to tell him.

"Roz, don't forget that we are leaving tomorrow," Yolanda stressed. "No if's, and's, or but's.

"I know you really didn't want to stay, but I think Hamp could be the one." I explained.

"What time are you hookin' up?" she asked.

"It's supposed to be around 7'o clock," I said. "He is going to call me."

7'o clock turned into 8'o clock. 8'o clock turned into 9' o clock. Then 9'o clock turned into 10'o clock and Hamp never

43

called. I was confused. Everything was discussed. He was going to call me, and we were going to spend our last night together, just the two of us. Yolanda had fallen asleep, and that's just how I wanted it to stay. The last thing I needed was her telling me that I told you so and we should have never changed our plans just because you were hot in the pants. Hamp never told me the exact hotel he was staying at therefore, for the next couple of hours, I called around the city looking for Hamp. I was so nervous. Something must have happened, because he would have called. Unfortunately, there were several different hotel locations for the one he was staying at. I strategized and called the locations that were close to the airport. I tried to whisper so Yolanda would not wake up, but she did.

"I fell asleep?" she said in a groggy voice. "What time is it?"
I didn't say anything because I knew the moment, I said something, I would begin to cry.

"Girl, it's 1'o clock and you're back?" she said surprisingly. "I wasn't expecting to see you until about 6 or 7 am."

I could barely muster up the strength, but I finally opened my mouth and told her.

"Yolanda, I never went anywhere," I said holding back the tears. "He never called. I have been sitting here for the last few hours, in between the tears, calling around trying to find him. How could he let me down like this?

"You probably wrote down the wrong hotel name," she said trying to be optimistic. "Or maybe he wrote the wrong number down. Just try to take your mind off it and get some sleep."

I couldn't take my mind off it. I was too worried to sleep, so I continued to make calls to different hotels. After several calls, I found him!

"Yes, do you have a person by the last name of Hamp registered?" I asked timidly.

"Yes, would you like me to connect you to the room," said the operator.

"Please." I quickly responded.

FINALLY, I could not believe it. I could not wait to talk to him and make sure everything was ok. The operator came back on because there was no answer. She asked if I wanted to be connected to voicemail, so I agreed.

"Hey Hamp, it's me Roz," I said softly. "I hope that everything is ok. I was expecting to hear from you by now. Please give me a call."

I sat there in the bed for the rest of the night waiting for his call. Our flight was leaving out at 10'o clock which meant we needed to leave the hotel no later than 8'o clock. I was praying that he would call so we could still spend some time together. I was so caught up in him, I was willing to catch a cab to wherever he was. Anything for one last chance to feel loved. It was now 3am and he still never called. I couldn't do anything but cry myself to sleep.

Beep, Beep, Beep, Beep…sounds the alarm clock. 6'o clock am, time to get up and get ready. My eyes were swollen because I had cried so much during the night. I didn't want to talk about anything. Yolanda obviously figured out that I never got a call because of my silence. She really didn't try to strike up a conversation nor make me talk. I got myself together and all packed up, while Yolanda went to check out. I was so desperate to talk to Hamp that I called the hotel one last time.

"Yes, can you connect me with Mr. Hamp?" I asked while praying that there would be an answer this time.

"Hello," a strange voice answered.

"Can I speak to Hamp?" I waited patiently. I could hear people in the background, both male and female. It sounded like they were all wide awake.

"Yeah, this is Hamp." He said cheerfully.

"Hamp, it's Roz," I said trying not to cry. "What happened?

"What do you mean what happened?" He said cluelessly.

"We were supposed to get together last night remember?" hoping the light bulb would go off soon. "I am leaving today." I explained.

"Me and the fellas went out last night and I guess I forgot about the time." He said.

"Hamp, I called the hotel that you gave me, and you weren't there," I began to cry. "Then, I realized you didn't give me the specific hotel, so I had to call around and find you. Then when I called the operator told me there was no answer, so I left a

message. What happened? I gave you the number here to this
hotel, why didn't you call me?

"Well we can still get together today," He said like it was no big
deal. "Why are you so upset?"

"Hamp, I changed my plans just for you," I stated. "I paid money
to change the flight and I lied to my parents. "Yolanda's mom
even had a party planned for her that she had to rearrange for
tonight. Who is that I hear in the background? How many of you
are in that room?"

"It was me, Johnson, Lewis and a few other friends." He got quiet.

"Hamp, I hear females in the background, who is that?" I
demanded.

"Roz, look, don't get upset," He explained. "Nothing happened,
it's was just a few friends from Charlie Company that we knew."
Now, it doesn't take a genius to figure this one out. I know better
because the first night we spent together it was just him Johnson,
Lewis and a few of my friends. I could not believe that I didn't see
it coming. He was so convincing. I thought that he really cared
about me. I got played like a funky piano.

"Look, Roz, I can meet you somewhere and we can talk," he said,
"or you can come over here."

"Hamp, Yolanda is downstairs checking out right now," I tried to
speak as clearly as possible. "My plane leaves in 2 hours. What do
you want me to do?

"Call me when you get home tonight," he said. "I leave this
afternoon and I should be home by 8'o clock tonight."

By this time, Yolanda had already come back in the room and I was so glad because I needed a shoulder to cry on. She didn't say I told you so, but what she did say I can't put in this book. Anyway, she was there for me and told me that everything was going to be alright. I wanted to believe her. We had a great flight home, and everybody was so glad to see us. Unfortunately, I couldn't get Hamp off my mind. I was laughing and talking, but on the inside, I was heart-broken. Yolanda's mom was giving her a coming home party, but I didn't even go. I just wanted to go home.

Once I got home and settled, I watched the clock to make sure I didn't miss calling Hamp. He told me to call around 8'o clock. I tried not to be too anxious, so at 8:05 pm I decided to call. "Hello, may I speak to Hamp, oh I mean Eric?" I said happily "Sweetie he is not home yet." she said very motherly. "Ok, thank-you." I quickly hung up the phone. I just decided to wait until he called. I was sure that it would be tonight.

A few days passed, and I still never heard from Hamp. I decided to give it another try. This time he answered the phone. "Hey, it's Roz," I said with excitement in my voice. "Whatcha doin?"

"Nothing much, just getting used to being back home," he said. "What about you?"

"Well, I was thinking about you," I said. "I miss you."

He did not respond. He never said that he missed me or anything close to it. I tried to play it off and change the subject.

"You know Mardi Gras is in a couple of days," I said. "You've never seen it?"

"No." he stated.

"Well, I don't usually get all into it, but I will take pictures of the floats and weird costumes and send them to you." I was hoping this would get the conversation going.

"Ok." he said.

We held the phone only for a few more minutes before he said he would call me back. I already knew not to sit by the phone this time. Instead I decided to write him a letter telling him how I feel. I was going to include it with the Mardi Gras pictures.

I remember taking pictures of anything weird that Fat Tuesday. I really wanted Hamp to get an idea of what Mardi Gras was like. We lived one block away from where the Truck parade passed. So, you could see everything from the front porch. At one point, when my mom came outside, I even asked her to take pictures of me in front of cool floats. I was acting like I was a model at a photo shoot, because I was trying to make all kinds of faces and poses. It was crazy. The next day I rushed to the drugstore, got the pictures developed and mailed the best ones off to Hamp. I couldn't wait to hear what he thought about the pictures and the letter I wrote. I finally told him that I loved him, and I couldn't wait to come to Washington to visit.

In the meantime, Yolanda and I were busy trying to apply to local colleges for the upcoming semester. Things were a lot different when I got back, because I had a lot more freedom. I was able to finally go out. If I wasn't at home, I was at Yolanda's house. She and I had been through so much with basic training and AIT school and heartbreaks, we had become the best of friends, almost inseparable. After we spent the mornings taking care of business, we would go and work out at the military base. Both of us were trying to stay fine and fit thanks to the drill sergeant almost killing us every morning at 5:00am. I just knew I wanted to look good for Hamp the next time we saw each other.

About a week after I sent Hamp the pictures and my letter he finally called. We had a good conversation talking about the weird things that go on at Mardi Gras. He had already met with his career officer and the wheels were in motion for him working at the Pentagon. I was anxious to ask him about the letter, but I played it cool for the entire conversation without blurting it out too soon. Right when I was about to mention it, somebody beeped in and he needed to call me back. I just laid there on the bed thinking about the nights we spent together back in Carolina, and how wonderful everything was. I wanted to experience it all over again. After about 30 minutes he called back. This time I decided to bring up the letter before any more interruptions.

"Umm, Hamp, did you read the letter that I sent you," I waited patiently for a response.

"What letter?" he asked.

But before I could say something, I heard him laughing. I was relieved.

"Yeah, I got it," he said. "You were serious about what you said? You know about the way you feel?

"Of course," I said softly. "I love you."

There I finally said it. I had never said that to anybody before in my life, not even to anybody in my family. I waited patiently for his reply, but unfortunately, he was taking a little too long and the silence was a little obvious.

"Hamp, are you there?" I asked.

"Roz, I'm sorry," he started to explain. "I like you a lot but...

"But what." I said.

"I don't feel the same way," he said. "I liked what we had back in Carolina, but I don't think it can be anything more."

"What are saying," holding back the tears. "You said that we could make a long-distance relationship work. I thought you wanted me to come hang out with you in Washington." I held my breath until he spoke again.

"Roz, I don't think it's going to work," he announced. "Like I said, Carolina was good, but I've got to focus on my career."

"Sorry, I gotta go."

Hamp hung up the phone, while I sat on the bed wondering what just happened. I locked the door to my bedroom and cried softly in my pillow. How can somebody make you feel like you are the only girl that exist and then turn around and make you feel like you don't want to exist anymore? I keep falling for the wrong guy. The more and more I think that I have found him, the more wrong I am.

I called Yolanda and told her what had just happened. She came over and picked me, so we could go somewhere and talk. We went to the Daiquiri Shop and stayed for hours. Yolanda talked and drank, and I cried and drank. I felt so stupid. I poured out my heart to Hamp. It seemed like he was different from other guys, but he was just the same. Do all guys want to play games? I better figure out how to play the game before I get hurt again. I decided that I wasn't going to let anybody get close to me again. I was going to dog out the guy before he dogged me out. This way I don't need to get all caught up in that emotional crap ever again! After a few weeks, the disappointment of not being with Hamp got easier. No matter what Hamp thought, I knew that I was a good catch. I had the brains and beauty. I just needed to use them to my advantage. I was young and indestructible, so I thought.

One day, Yolanda and I were on base doing our weekly workout. We had just finished running and needed something to drink. Instead of moving the car, we decided to walk to the Px, which was just on the other side of the track. As we were walking, this fine brother in a smooth BMW passed us by. Immediately, I saw the brake lights go on and I looked at Yolanda. My dream car is the BMW, 325i series and still is. It is bold and strong. I always thought that car made a statement of "I have arrived." Besides, who could resist a beautiful black woman pushing a smooth black BMW? Anyway, enough about my car, back to the fine brother. I think I gave Yolanda a look, like you know that's my car, so let me get the play. She just looked like, we'll let him decide.

"Hey ladies," he said with a gorgeous smile. "Where y'all headed to?"

"We're just going to get something to drink," Yolanda answered. "We have been working out."

"Do you want a ride?" he asked.

I wanted to scream. This man was fine and could be talking to any chick on base, but he stopped to talk to us. Did he just ask if we wanted a ride in the BMW? I tried not to smile too much as we accepted the offer and got in the car. I had not said anything yet because it seemed like Yolanda had already tried to make a play on him.

Yolanda was very pretty, and she knew it. She had the good hair, so I thought, and beautiful fair skin. Me on the other hand, dark skin with glasses and there was no "Indian" in my family. I had the rough hair! I was always secretly jealous of her because of that. I always felt like I would have to compete against her for a guy's attention.

"So, what's your name?" he asked as we drove off.

"I'm Yolanda and this is Rosalind." she said.

"Rosalind," he said as if he was meditating on the sound of it. "Can I call you Roz?"

Oh-Oh, it seemed like the play was coming my way.

"Yeah, everybody calls me that." I said with a smile. "So, what's your name?"

"Spencer, well Ross Spencer," he said. "But everybody calls me Spence. I'm stationed here in New Orleans and I live on base. What branch are you guys in?"

"We're in the Army Reserves," I explained. "Yolanda and I just got back about two months ago from training. We have been coming on base a few days each week to work out and stay in shape."

"Well, you are doing a good job at it, trust me." he said.

He was very nice and talkative on the short ride to the Px. We all got out of the car and I noticed he was busy checking me out on the sly, as well as other females on base, but I was busy checking him out. Spence was in the Marines and he was looking good in that uniform.

He walked with so much confidence, like he knew he had it going on. He seemed like he should be on a toothpaste commercial, because when he smiled a shimmer of light beamed off his teeth. He was very smooth and dreamy. When we walked into the store, he told us to get whatever we wanted. He paid for everything and then gave us a quick tour around base before driving us to Yolanda's car.

"Ok ladies, front door service," as he pulled up right in front of the car.

"Thank you." Yolanda and I almost said at the exact same time.

"So, umm Roz," he hesitated a little. "Can I get your number? I would love to hook up with you guys the next time you come on base."

"Sure," I smiled as I gave him my number.

That's what happened. We would call each other before we came on the base and he would work out with us. I would love to watch his muscles flex on the equipment. He would always wear these biker shorts that emphasized his shapely body. After our run, we all would go to the Px and cool off with a drink.

One afternoon, Spence called and asked if I wanted to go swimming at his apartment complex. I was so excited because normally we would just work out together, make crazy jokes, have a few drinks, and that's all. I had never even been to his apartment.

"I'll call Yolanda and asked her what time we can be over there." I said.

"Can't you come over by yourself," he asked.

"No," I explained. "I couldn't even if I wanted to. I don't have my own transportation yet. Besides, I would not feel right if Yolanda wasn't there and she found out somehow."

"I don't want your girl to feel left out." Spence stated.

"Well she won't if you get on the phone and call a few of your friends over to entertain her." I said as if I had solved the mystery. He agreed to Yolanda coming over. He also told me to explain to Yolanda that some of his friends were also going to be at his house. I called Yolanda and she was excited about going, not to mention meeting some of his Marine buddies. After making a quick stop at the mall for a bathing suit, we finally made it to Spence's house.

His apartment was nice, very bachelor style. He really didn't show us around his apartment, but I checked it out while I was bringing some snacks outside. Spence was cooking on the grill and Yolanda and I were lounging by the pool drinking wine coolers. About thirty minutes, almost an hour had passed and none of his friends had arrived yet.

"Roz," Yolanda whispered. "I thought you said that Spence was going to have some of his friends over here? I feel like a third wheel. Go ask him, where are they?"

"No," I hesitated. "He's acting kinda weird to me, don't you think? I mean he is just usually a little more talkative."

"Girl he's full of that beer," Yolanda hinted. "He's been drinking non-stop since we walked in the door. He has also been checking you out a lot. So, he's not going to be to talkative because he is enjoying the show."

Yolanda was right about Spence drinking a lot. He was putting those beers down left and right. If he wasn't grabbing for a beer, he was doing shots. He didn't really talk to Yolanda a lot. He mainly focused on me and the alcohol. I just tried to enjoy his company and talk to Yolanda, so she would not feel so left out. After we ate and played around in the pool, we all stretched out on the lounge chairs and relaxed. Eventually we all dozed off. I woke a little while later because I needed to use the bathroom. I hated to wake up Spence, but I didn't know where he put the keys to his apartment.

"Spence...Spence," I whispered as I gently shoved him. "Where are your keys? "I need to use the bathroom."

"Look under those towels by the pool," he said. "Are you getting ready to leave?"

"No," I replied. "I just need to use the bathroom. I probably will change because I'm not getting back into the pool. Besides Yolanda is still sleeping and I can't wait until she wakes up."

"Ok...good." he replied. "I'm going to start bringing some of the food upstairs. Leave the door unlocked. I'll be right behind you."

I slipped on my shoes and headed upstairs.

As I was in the bathroom, I heard Spence come inside. I quickly finished in the bathroom and came out. Spence was standing right there outside the bathroom door.

"Boy, you scared me!" I screamed. "What are you doing?"

I noticed Spence changed out of his wet swim trunks into some boxers. He had this strange look on his face.

"I'm just waiting for you." he said in a very subtle voice. "You know, I forgot to tell you that you look really good in that bathing suit. I'm glad you didn't change yet."

"I forgot my bag in the other room, because I had to use the bathroom so bad," I explained. "Can you go get it for me. It's the small pink bag in the first room."

"You don't need to change so fast," he insisted. "Give me a hug."

I gave Spence a hug, but the smell of all that beer was making me sick. After we hugged, he pulled me over to the couch. It was obvious to me that Spence was trying to make his move. He was touching and rubbing me all over, but he wasn't gentle. He was being very aggressive and rough. This was the first time Spence and I had ever really been alone with each other. I knew that he was digging on me and I felt the same, but he was acting very strange that I was feeling uncomfortable. Before I knew it, he kissed me. His tongue was so far down my throat I thought I was going to choke.

"Spence!" I called. "What's the matter with you? Come on. Yolanda is going to wake up and wonder what happened to us." I really wasn't worried about Yolanda. I just tried to make up any excuse to get him to snap out of it. But Spence was in another zone.

"Come on Roz," he said in a smooth low voice. "This will only take a minute. I need to feel it."

"No Spence," I said. "I really don't want to do this." Let's go back to the pool. Yolanda is out there all by herself."

Spence was like another person. He grabbed me by the shoulders and pushed me down on the couch. Then he laid on top of me. I felt like I could not breathe. He was a big guy. Spence weighed about 250 lbs. and he was in great physical shape. I punched him on his chest as hard as I could. I tried to move him off me, but it was impossible! He trapped me on the couch with his body weight. He was trying to force himself inside of me. I could not believe this was happening!

"Spence...stop..." I cried. "You are too rough. Get off me."

"You know you want some of this," he said in a chauvinistic way. "I saw how you been lookin' at me, so stop acting like you don't want it."

He kept forcing himself inside of me with one hand while he held me down with his other hand. The only thing I could do was keep pleading with him to stop. I felt helpless and paralyzed. He was so overpowering, it felt useless to fight...

After a while, there was a knock at the door.

Knock...Knock...Knock...

"Open the door, it's Yolanda," she said unsuspectingly. "Y'all didn't have to wake me up. Just leave me out there all by myself. Hurry up, I need to go to the bathroom."

I was so relieved to hear her voice. But Spence didn't stop. He covered my mouth and gave me this strange look, so I would not yell. He was determined to finish. The more Yolanda knocked and called out, the more forceful he became to reach his peak.

I called out to Yolanda, so she would stop banging on the door.

"Ok Yolanda, were coming." I tried to say in my normal voice. Soon it was all over, even though it felt like hours. Spence rolled off me and fixed his shorts.

"Don't say nothing," he said in a stern voice. "Get up and go clean yourself up."

I ran into the bathroom and began to cry very quietly. I couldn't believe what just happened. He just took advantage of me. He raped me!

I was just sitting on the toilet for a few minutes asking myself if what just happened really happened. I was debating if I should run out and tell Yolanda or not. What should I do? What would he do if I said something? I was scared and confused. I just wanted to leave.

Outside the bathroom door, I could hear Yolanda and Spence talking and laughing.

"Why y'all didn't wake me up?" she asked. "I jumped up and looked around and saw a bunch of people I didn't know."

"Those were just other people who live here in the complex," he said in a calm voice. "You're a big girl."

"Ha ha… very funny," she laughed. "Where's Roz? "But more importantly, why didn't you open the door sooner? I told you I had to go to the bathroom."

"You have a lot of questions for somebody that just woke up," he said. "Roz and I just came up here because she had to go to the bathroom too. I'm going to change my clothes."

I heard Spence walk down the hall. I waited for his door to close before I came out of the bathroom. I didn't want to even look at him. I dried my eyes and took a deep breath before I came out of the bathroom. I decided not to say anything and act normal.

Yolanda was in the kitchen getting a drink when I came out of the bathroom.

"I'm glad you're out," she said. "I need to use the bathroom very badly."

I didn't respond to Yolanda. I just walked to the couch and turned on the television. Spence was still in his room. I could not hear any sounds coming from there. I wondered what he was doing. Was he regretting what just happened? I kept replaying the last fifteen minutes over in my mind. Why didn't I scream or yell for help? Why didn't I kick and scratch? I felt like such a fool for not fighting back more.

Maybe Spence was right, I thought. Maybe I did want him. I was fascinated with his BMW and his body. He probably did see me checking him out. Maybe I did ask for it? But I told him to stop, I thought. I was going back and forth with all kinds of thoughts in my mind. It was making my head spin so much that I couldn't take it anymore.

"Yo, what's taking you so long?" I asked. "Are you ready to go yet? It's getting late.

"Yeah, just about." she responded.

When Yolanda came out of the bathroom, I was in the kitchen getting a beer. I knew that if I drank enough, I could forget what just happened and feel mellow and calm. She walked right over to me and just stared.

"What's the matter with you?" she asked.

Yolanda and I had spent everyday day together for the last 8 or 9 months. She knew me very well and how to read my emotions.

"Nothing," I stated. "Let's just go."

"Something is wrong," she said. "Where's Spence?"

As she was asking where Spence was, he walked out of his room. I got nervous. What was he about to say?

"I'm hungry," he smiled. "Do y'all want me to put some more burgers on the grill?"

He was fine. Spence was being Spence. He had changed his clothes and was talking about food. I could barely look at him. All I wanted to do was get the hell out of there. Yolanda knew that I wanted to leave so she took charge of the conversation.

"No, it's getting late." Yolanda said. "We're about to go."

"Ok." he said, as he fixed another plate of food. "Y'all need me to walk you to your car?"

"Nope, it's right out front." she said.

We grabbed our bags and started walking out the door. Spence acted like everything was fine. He even told us that he would see us tomorrow at our usually time on base at the gym. I closed the door and knew that was the last time I would see Spence. He was just like all the others. He didn't care about me or how I felt.

I was almost dreading getting in the car with Yolanda because I knew that she was going to ask me what happened.

"Ok Roz, what's the matter?" she asked in a concerned voice. "You were acting weird back there. What's wrong?"

I decided at that moment that I could not tell Yolanda what happened. What if Spence was right? Maybe I did want it. I was checkin' him out and trippin' about the BMW. Maybe I gave him a sign that it was ok. I just wanted to forget everything that happened. This would be my secret.

"I wasn't acting weird," I said in my normal voice. "I was just a little upset because Spence lied.

"Oh, you mean about his friends being over there?" Yolanda asked.

"Yeah," I said sadly. "Maybe if his friends were there things would have been different. I wish you didn't have to be by yourself. What he did was not cool at all. I think that's going to be the end Spence."

"Just because he didn't have friends over there for me?" You trippin'," she said. "I thought that you liked him. Girl, that man got a BMW! I don't know what's wrong with you but are acting crazy. What happened Roz?"

"Spence is an idiot!" I stressed. "He didn't invite his friends over there on purpose. He wanted to be alone with me!"

After a few seconds of silence, Yolanda finally asked the question. "So, you and him..." she implied.

"No!" I interrupted. "Spence just finished telling me why his friends never came right before you knocked on the door. I was so ticked off with him that I just wanted to leave. He's not worth it."

Days turned into weeks as I tried to forget about Spence and how he took advantage of me. I kept replaying that afternoon over and over in my head, wondering what I could have done differently. No matter what I thought, it happened, and I could not turn back the clock. Eventually Yolanda and I just exercised in the park, so we could avoid me seeing him again. Ironically, after everything I tried to do to avoid Spence, I still saw him again. It was a long time, at least a year before I saw him again, but he had not changed.

I was going to pay for some traffic tickets at the court house one day and Spence was there. He didn't even recognize me! I was walking through the crowded lobby to get to Section B and there was a long line of people against the wall waiting to make payment arrangements. I saw the military uniform, but the persons back were turned towards me. As I got closer, he turned around and smiled. I made eye contact with him and almost screamed. It was Spence! It was like I saw a ghost. He leaned over at just the right time to grab my hand.

"Say baby, he said in a smooth voice. "What's your name? Can I get your number and call you sometime?"

Instantly, all those bad memories came back. I couldn't believe he was serious. I didn't even bother to answer him. I looked at him for seconds, read his name tag to make sure I wasn't dreaming and shook my head in confusion. I snatched my hand out of his and walked off in disgust. I looked back and he was leaning over the rails checking me out. He never realized that it was me. This brought me back to that afternoon in his apartment. How many other females did he do this to? Apparently, there must have been plenty for him not to recognize me. I was just another score in his book. But this was another scar in my life that I continued to bury.

Rebound

I finally received an acceptance letter from a local university. It had been months since I heard from Spelman, so I decided to move on and re-channel my energy elsewhere. Yolanda also got accepted into a great school, but on the other side of town. This meant we could only hook up on the weekends. My life seemed very boring from my point of view. I went to class, studied in the library for about 1 hour, then straight home for the rest of the day. I wanted some excitement. Then, one day, while I was on my way home, something happened.

As I was waiting for the bus, a car drove by and blew the horn. This happens all the time to most females who are outside walking, sitting, standing, whatever, it happens, so I did not pay any attention to the person or the car. A few seconds later, a car pulled up to the curb and stopped.

"Excuse me," the person yelled from the car. "Are you going home?"

I was going over some notes from class, so I never looked up to who the person was talking to.

"Are you going to make me sit here and burn up my gas?" he said. "Or would you like a ride home?"

Nobody else at the bus stop was responding to the person in the car, so I decided to look up. I couldn't believe my eyes. It was Johnathan, the doctor from the morning bus ride. I shook my head in disbelief and quickly picked up my bags and headed for the car. I had not seen Johnathan since before I left for the military last year.

"Johnathan, what are you doing here?" I asked with a huge smile on my face.

"I work at a clinic in the evening right up the street," he said. "This is the route I take going home. Well are you going to stand there, or do you want a ride home? I remember where you live."

I thought about it for a brief second and then I immediately got in the car. Johnathan was always a gentleman since the day I met him. He was the kind of person I would love to call my man.

I could not believe that I was riding in the same car with him. I had a secret crush on him for several years now.

"So how was everything?" he asked. "I see you made it. And you managed to still look good."

"It was an experience," I explained. "Yolanda and I learned a lot."

"Now, who is Yolanda again?" he asked.

"She was my classmate from school," I said. "She and I have become the best of friends. We are pretty much inseparable on the weekends."

"Speaking of weekends, what do you have planned?" he asked.

I was about to scream. Johnathan, the man I have had a crush on since high school was about to ask me out. I could not believe this was happening. I tried my best to be cool and play it off like it was not a big deal.

"I really don't have any plans right now, but I'm sure Yolanda and I will come up with something." I said.

"Is your mom's telephone number the same?" he asked.

"Actually, it is, but I have my own telephone now." I said proudly. I took out a piece of paper and wrote down the new number. Johnathan slipped it into his pocket and smiled. I could not believe he was still interested after all this time.

For the next few days, Johnathan and I spent a lot of time talking on the phone. I loved talking to him. He would always try to offer his advice or guidance in a gentle way. I would ask him about college, careers, and other things. No matter what we talked about, he would always remind me that he was older and had the better answer or solution. I thought he was so mature. I was just amazed that he would even take the time to talk to me.

Johnathan was a good looking, successful doctor and could have any female he wanted, instead he spent his afternoons bringing me home from class and his nights talking on the phone with me. Strange? Yes, I thought. Why? I wasn't sure at first, but I knew that we had a good chemistry brewing. I felt in my heart that he enjoyed my presence as much as I enjoyed his. He would always say that I was a woman trapped inside a young girl's body. Even though he was 12 years older than me, we had a good friendship.

"So, where's your girlfriend Johnathan?" I finally got the nerve to ask.

"I don't have one." he commented.

"Stop playing," I laughed. "I know there is somebody you're involved with."

"Seriously there is nobody," he explained. "I really don't have time with my schedule. Most ladies I meet want me to spend all my money on them. Some of them think I'm snobby, just because I'm a doctor and the rest think I'm arrogant. I just haven't met somebody who liked me for me yet. I just want to be with somebody who likes having fun. Sometimes I feel like I missed out because I went straight from high school, then to college and then medical school. Immediately after med school, I began studying for the MCAT and now I'm working. Don't get me wrong, she must be intelligent. I don't want a dumb woman. And I want her to be successful or working towards a goal. I want us to be in the same 'class.' What about you? Where's your boyfriend?"

"I don't have a boyfriend," I said. "I had a few bad experiences, so now I'm just waiting for the right one. I want excitement, intelligent conversations, spontaneity, and goal-oriented. Most guys these days can't give me that.

"So, you mean to tell me you are not involved with anybody." he asked.

"That's what I said," I answered. "Why is that so hard to believe? You're not involved either. Oh, I forgot. That's because you're snobby and arrogant.

"That's very funny." he said.

He introduced me to fine wine, fancy restaurants and high society events. Me, Inmate 222, I felt I had finally arrived.

"Yolanda, guess what?" I said about to burst with excitement. "Johnathan asked me to a Fund Raiser this Friday night."

"First of all, you have been talking to the Johnathan for the past few weeks and I have not met him yet, " she said. "When am I going to meet him and girl what's so exciting about a Fund Raiser?" she asked.

"It is to benefit the current Mayor in his re-election efforts!" I exclaimed. "It is a black-tie affair and it will be at the Mayor's home."

"Why did he ask you?" she said. "Are you guys dating? You didn't tell me."

"No, we're not dating," I explained. "We are just good friends. I know Johnathan could have asked anybody, but he asked me! Can you believe it? He is just a great guy and I like him a lot, but he doesn't know it. We spend a lot of time talking about college, different careers. He is a good friend, but I wouldn't mind if it turned into something else. Well look I have a lot to do, so I will talk to you later. And don't worry, I told him about you, and he knows that you are my girl. You'll meet him real soon, with his gorgeous self. I'll talk to you later."

I spent the rest of the week preparing and shopping for just the right outfit. I could barely sleep thinking about all the important political figures I was going to meet. Johnathan was cool every time I talked to him, but he had no clue about my excitement.

"Johnathan what if somebody asks me how old I am?" I asked in a concern voice. "I'm only 19! What if they ask something that I am not familiar with?"

"Roz, why are you so nervous?" he said. "I am going to be right there with you the entire night. I would not have asked you if I didn't think you could handle it. Besides, this will be good exposure for you since you are interested in law school. I'll pick you up around 6 o'clock Friday and we'll get a few cocktails before we go."

I spent the entire afternoon in the bathroom getting ready. I wanted everything to be just right. Johnathan and I hung out before, but never anything like this. He pulled up a little after six and our night began. I walked to the car praying that what I was wearing was appropriate and that Johnathan would approve. He just told me to look classy.

"Hey Johnathan," I said nervously. "How are you?"

He didn't say anything. At least he didn't say anything right away. He was looking at me in shock. I didn't know if it was good or bad. I decided not to say anything.

"Ummm Roz," he hesitated. "You look good. No, I mean you look great, very classy. We're going to stop at my house for a drink or two and then we'll head over to the Mayor's house. And remember, I don't want you to be nervous. I will be right there with you the entire night."

This was like a dream come true for me. I was riding in a top of the line Beamer, with a good-looking successful brother on my way to a gala for the Mayor. I felt like royalty. This is what I have been wanting to experience all my life.

I had loosened up a lot on the drive over the Mayor's house. Johnathan was very reassuring. Until he commented on my hands. You see, my outfit was a tuxedo pant suit, just right for that bold, classy statement. It was obviously black and white, and I couldn't find the right nail polish, so I polished my nails black. I thought it was fine, but apparently Johnathan didn't approve.

"Roz," he said in a very concerned tone. "Your nails are black. Black.

"I know, black goes perfect with my outfit," I explained. "Is it ok?"

"Their black," he said. "I have never seen anybody with black nails.

I felt so stupid at this point. I was trying to make a good impression on Johnathan, and his circle of friends and I blew it.

"Roz," he said in a mellow voice. "That's sexy! I never said I didn't like it. I am just shocked because I never saw anything like it. You are so different. That's what I like about you."

I just smiled in relief and knew that this was going to be a great night. When we arrived, Johnathan did exactly what he said.

He stayed with me the entire night, acting as some sort of body guard. There were a few stares from some people, but nobody asked my age. I gave my firm hand shake when needed, and expressed my interest in the political race. It was great. Several times throughout the night Johnathan would whisper in my ear, "your nails are black." We both smiled at each other and went back to our conversations. Johnathan didn't see age when he looked at me. He appreciated me for an intelligent female. He exposed me to fine wine, nice cars, and fancy restaurants. I didn't want the night to end.

"Well that was nice," Johnathan said as we walked back to the car. "You did fine. I think you even impressed a few of my friends."

"I just tried to be Roz," I said. "…you know, I really had a good time. Thanks for giving me the opportunity to experience it."

"What time do you have to be home?" he asked.

"I really don't have a curfew anymore," I said. "Things have lightened up a bit since I got back, why?"

"Well, I was thinking we could go back to my house for a little while." he suggested.

"Ok, for a little while." I agreed.

I was jumping up and down on the inside. He wanted to spend more time with me. He always treated me with respect, so I felt very comfortable with being with him.

We went back to his house and talked until 2am. I was in heaven. He never tried anything. Once we realized how late it was getting Johnathan decided to bring me home.

"Do you want to do something tomorrow?" he asked.

"Yeah, that sounds good," I said. "Maybe we can get together with Yolanda and her boyfriend. I have been wanting you to meet her.

"That's cool," he said. "We can just get something to eat and hang out at my house. "I'll pick you up around 2 o'clock."

When we got to my house, he walked me to the door and gave me a kiss on the check. I thought that was so romantic. I knew that tomorrow was going to be an even better day.

I called Yolanda and woke her up early Saturday morning to tell her about my evening. She was happy for me. I even told her that Johnathan invited us all over to his house to hang and get to know each other. I gave her the address and told her to be there around 3 o'clock.

As he said, Johnathan picked me up at 2 o'clock and we headed back to his place. We were still laughing and joking about my "black fingernails." I was really falling head over heels for Johnathan. The last few weeks, I shared with him my experiences in high school and the military, well almost everything. I didn't tell him about Spence. Anyway, he knew that I was looking for a special person, but I don't think he had any idea that I wanted that person to be him. Johnathan knew that I was much younger than him and he did mention that he wanted a relationship, but he just could not find the right girl. It was weird because both of us were looking for a relationship. We developed a close friendship and we encouraged each other all the time on meeting that special someone.

I wanted to be that special someone. I knew that I could make this relationship work.   Yolanda and Aaron arrived at the house around 3:30ish. I was so excited about her meeting Johnathan. I wanted to get her opinion of him. I decided to go outside and meet them at the car.

"Heyyy girrrl!" we both said in unison.

"Hey Aaron, what's going on?" I said. "What took you guys so long?"

"We decided to stop and get some cards and board game we could play," Yolanda explained. "Well, where is he? I have been waiting to meet this Johnathan. I want to know who's been taking my friend away from me!"

"Girl stop playing," I said "He's inside, com'on. Now remember, we are just friends."

It was very weird because I acted like Johnathan was my parent and I was trying to make a good impression.

"Johnathan, this is my girl Yolanda and her friend, Aaron." I said with excitement.

"Hello, nice to finally meet you," he said extending his hand. "Roz talks about you a lot."

"Well that's good to know since I haven't talked to her on the phone that much in the past few weeks," she said. "I thought she forgot about me. Humm, I wonder why I haven't talked to her on the phone? Apparently, something has her attention."

I thought I was going to scream. That was Yolanda's way of telling me, girl this man is fine. I need to hook y'all up!

We spent the rest of the afternoon, playing silly board games, and joking around. It seemed liked everybody was getting along great. Then Yolanda and Aaron were headed out. Before they left, Yolanda found a way to give me a look of approval. I just wanted to play it cool and follow Johnathan's lead. Whichever direction he wanted to take with the relationship was going to be fine with me. I walked them to the car, then headed back inside with a huge smile on my face.

"What are you so happy about?" he asked.

"I'm just glad you got a chance to meet Yolanda." I said.

"So, this Aaron guy," he hesitated. "Are they serious? He seemed a little distant at times.

"Well him and Yolanda are together one week and break up the next week," I explained. "It's been like that for a while. But he is crazy about her. I don't know. Maybe this was one of their off weeks.

"You never told me how pretty she was." Johnathan said with expectation in his voice. "She is even the shorter than me.

It was very rare that Johnathan would meet a girl that was shorter than him. You see, Johnathan was not the average 6'0" tall guy. Instead he was about 5'5". He shared this to me in a few of our conversations about his height being one of the reasons he didn't have a girlfriend. A lot of females don't want a guy who is shorter than them. Johnathan was so good looking and intelligent that it didn't bother me at all. I was hoping that he would realize his height was not an issue for me and that I was the girl he had been looking for. Wait a minute! Why was he asking about Yolanda?

"Roz, you've been holding out on me." he smiled. "Yolanda would be perfect for me."

On the outside I was smiling and listening, but on the inside, I was screaming

NOOOOOOOOOOOOOOOOOOOOOOOOOOOOOOOOOOOOOOOOOOOOOOOOOOOOOOO! My heart dropped. I could not believe what I was hearing. I had been head-over-heels for this man since 9th grade and here we are 4 years later in his home after spending countless hours on the phone, going to high society affairs, laughing, joking, sharing and this MAN tells me that he thinks my best FRIEND is perfect for him! Why? Why? Why? Could it get any worse?

"Roz, can you try to hook us up?" he suggested.

It just got worse! Suddenly, I was numb. Johnathan didn't even realize that I had feelings for him. I had been playing it safe, trying not to rush into any relationship to fast after my past experiences. I decided I was not going to tell him how I felt, instead just let things happen. It all felt right. It all seemed like it was going in the right direction until that Saturday afternoon. It took everything inside of me not to break down and cry. Even though I was devastated, I sucked it up until I got home.

"Johnathan, you know Yolanda and Aaron are involved with each other," I tried to explain. "And besides, how do you know that she's your type?"

"Roz she is beautiful," he said. "Just see if you could drop her a few good lines about me and I'll do the rest. I don't want to seem too anxious, so maybe we can wait until next weekend and get together again."

"I'll see what I can do." I said.

I was devastated. I wanted to tell him so badly that I was the girl for him, but I didn't want to risk ruining our relationship. Was he that blind, I thought? Johnathan had to have known that I was interested in him, but once he saw Yolanda, all that went out of the window.

"Well you better get me home, so I can start working on this." I said.

"Ok," he replied. "Do you want to get together tomorrow and do something?

"I'll let you know." I said.

Making plans with Johnathan was the last thing on my mind right now. I just wanted to get home. I had cried enough in the past over bad relationships, and I did not want to cry anymore. Instead, I found myself staring in the mirror trying to figure out what was wrong with me. How come every guy that I am interested in does not have the same feelings for me? I was not dumb. Learning came very easy for me. I was not boring. I loved to laugh, joke and have fun.

It must have been my looks. I didn't see myself as the prettiest girl in the world. I did not have a nice grain of hair, like most guys liked. I did have hair, thank God, but nothing to brag about. I had a big nose, hairy legs, and still wearing the same bra size since 7th grade. In other words, NO BREASTS WHATSOEVER! And to top it all off, I wore glasses. I had been wearing glasses since the 1st grade. I thought about contacts, but I never got up the courage to do it. I tried to wear up-to-date clothes at low prices, but maybe it was still noticeable. I think this was the moment that I began hating myself. I was willing to do anything to be loved by somebody. Even if it meant trying to hook up Yolanda with Johnathan, just hoping that he would realize I was the one. I decided to call and tell her the big news.

"Hey Yolanda, whatcha doing?" I said trying to sound normal.

"Just sitting here waiting for you to call," she said with excitement.

"Ok, I know you already know what I am about to say, but I'll say it anyway. Johnathan is HOT! I think you and he make a great couple. You and he seem to get along just like a couple."

"You think so?" I asked. "Well, I have something to tell you that you won't believe."

"Girl what is it?" she asked very eagerly. "Are you two officially dating?He gave you a key to his house?"

"No, nothing like that," I said trying to calm her down. "This is very hard for me to say. I can't believe that I am about to say it."

"Say what?" she asked.

"Johnathan, apparently, you made a great first impression on him and he thinks you are cute."

For a moment there was a dead silence on the phone. The only thing that could be heard was the sniffling on my end, because I was upset. I was upset because Johnathan was attracted to Yolanda and not me. I was even more upset at myself, because I was jealous of Yolanda. She never had to work hard to get a guy. She would just enter a room and get all the attention, even when she wasn't trying, it still happened. I loved Yolanda like a sister and I was determined this would not come in between our friendship.

"Roz, what are you talking about?" she asked in a concerned voice. "I don't want Johnathan."

"I didn't say that you wanted him," I stressed. "I said he thinks you're cute. He is also blown away that you're short. Look, I know it sounds crazy, but it's the truth. He wanted me to drop some hints that he was interested, but I had to tell you everything."

"Do you like him Roz?" she asked.

"Of course, I do," I said. "But he is not interested in me."

"I guess not," she shouted. "You never told him how you feel! How is he supposed to know?"

"We are friends," I explained. "We get along really good and we are able to talk about anything. But he doesn't see me as a girlfriend. I am just not his type."

"Well, I don't know what he is going to do because I am not interested," she said. "And hello, didn't he see me there with Aaron."

"Yeah, but you know y'all are off and on," I hinted. "Besides, I know you think he is cute."

"I'm not blind!" she stated. "Of course, he's cute, but he is not my type. I don't want to sit around talking all that intellectual stuff. And it wouldn't matter anyway because you want him. That means my hands are off. Now what are you going to do?"

"Yolanda, I am not going to do anything," I explained. "I am just going to continue being there for him as a friend. I can't tell him how I feel. Well look, he wants to get together next weekend and hang out again. I think he is going to try and do his thing. What do you want me to tell him?"

"We can hang out," she explained. "I don't care, but you can let him know that I am not interested."

The next couple of days I tried not to call Johnathan as much. I just needed to take a break from our nightly calls. When he did call, I made sure that I was busy and told him I would call him back. I hated to lie, but I was still trying to absorb what happened. As the weekend drew near, he asked if we were still getting together and despite my inside screaming no, I agreed.

"Roz, what time is Yolanda coming over?" Johnathan asked.

"I told her 3o'clock" I answered.

"Do you think she will be interested in me?" he asked.

My Story, My Testimony, My Deliverance

It took everything inside of me to answer Johnathan. But who was I fooling. He obviously didn't look at me as a girlfriend. I tried to stay as quiet as possible and let him answer his own questions. I just shrugged my shoulders.

"Why wouldn't she be?" he said answering his own question. "I am a successful, good looking doctor. I own my home. I drive a great car. I could shower her with great gifts. I think we will make a great couple. Why are you so quiet?"

"Oh, no reason." I said. "I was just listening to you go on and on. Just be yourself."

"You know you're right," he said. "Thanks for listening. You know I have not been this excited about anybody in a long time. My history with women just hasn't been that great. Many of them think that I'm just a boring, snobby rich kid. I just have high standards."

As Johnathan was rattling on, the doorbell rang. It was Yolanda and Aaron. I was surprised that she asked Aaron to come since she knew that Johnathan was going to make a play on her. I noticed the disappointment on Johnathan's face as he saw both approach the door.

"Hey y'all," I said with excitement.

I think I was more excited to see Aaron than I was to see Yolanda. Maybe there could still be a chance for me and Johnathan.

"Yo, where's your car?" I asked.

"Girl, it was making this strange sound, so my dad decided to work on it," she explained. "Aaron and I caught the bus over here."

"How are you going to get home?" I asked.

Before Yolanda had a chance to open her mouth, Johnathan seized the opportunity.

"I can bring you home," he offered. "I can bring both of you home. Once I drop off Roz, I can bring Aaron home and then drop you off Yolanda."

It was obvious Johnathan was determined to try and get to know Yolanda. The rest of the afternoon, he made sure that he laughed at all of Yolanda jokes. If she asked a question, he made sure he had the perfect answer. He was not letting anything pass him by. The entire time, Aaron didn't realize what was going and I was just trying to be Roz. I was still disappointed about Johnathan wanting to be with Yolanda, but what was I going to do about it. If he didn't see me in that manner, what should I do? I decided that I would be very responsive to all his questions, and jokes, just as he was with Yolanda.

"Com'on y'all, let's play Truth or Dare," Aaron said.

We all were having a good time, laughing, drinking and hoping we didn't get a "dare" card, until Johnathan took the playing a bit too far. I don't know if it was him or the alcohol talking.

"Ok, Yolanda it's your turn," Johnathan said. "Pull a card."

It was a truth card. This was going to be interesting because it was Johnathan's turn to give Yolanda a "truth."

"Yolanda, do you like sex?" Johnathan asked.

I was in shock that he had enough nerve to ask that with Aaron sitting right their besides Yolanda. The next three cards that Yolanda pulled were "truth" cards, therefore, Johnathan was obviously using this as an opportunity to feel Yolanda out and what she likes and dislikes in a guy. He asked questions about sex, money and physical appearance. Every time I pulled a card, I gave responses that Johnathan would hopefully notice about what I liked and disliked in a guy. It was crazy because he wanted Yolanda's attention and I desperately wanted his attention. But what was weirder is that Aaron had no idea that Johnathan wanted his girl. If he did, he acted clueless. And what man you know is going to let somebody make a play on his girl right in front of his face?

"Johnathan, pull a card" Yolanda said.

He leaned in and pulled a card. It was a "dare" card.

"Ok, I dare you to take off your shirt" she said looking at me with a silly grin.

Johnathan hesitated for a few seconds, and then took it off. He looked good. I tried not to stare too much but it was hard not to look.

"My turn," I said trying to take the attention off Johnathan's chest. "It's a 'dare' card."

"I dare you to drink 2 beers in 1 minute." Aaron said.

"Cheers!" I said.

I finished the beers in less than a minute. Aaron and Johnathan were shocked, but Yolanda knew that I could drink. After a few minutes I was beginning to feel "really" good.

"Ok, my first 'dare' card. Com'on Johnathan, let's have it," Yolanda said.

"I dare you to kiss my chest." Johnathan said.

"Excuse me?" Yolanda asked. "I am not kissing your chest."

"What's the matter?" he asked. "I know you like it, or do you want to kiss something else? Don't be afraid... you probably kissed it before."

Now Johnathan had a few glasses of wine, but I don't think it was the wine talking. Johnathan knew exactly what he was saying to Yolanda. He was the type of guy that wanted a classy lady during the day and "freak" at night. Something else he shared with me about him desiring a girlfriend. I think he was trying to see how much information he could get out of her. Well he got it out of her.

SMACK! He got a serious slap across the face out of her!

"I don't play like that Johnathan!" she screamed. "What do you mean, do I want to kiss something else. What are you trying to say?"

"What the hell you hit me for?" Johnathan asked.

"Because you deserve it," Yolanda replied. "Look I'm outta here. Com'on Aaron let's go!"

"Yolanda don't go." I said.

"Roz, please don't." Yolanda stressed as she gathered her belongings.

I just sat there looking at Johnathan with this blank stare on my face. I could not believe what just happened. He totally disrespected Yolanda and Aaron. I gave him a serious look hinting he should say something before they leave. But then I remembered that Yolanda caught the bus to his house and she needed a ride home.

"Yolanda," I called. "Johnathan is taking you guys home. Let me put my shoes on and then we can go."

"Ok," she responded. "We'll be outside waiting."

I looked at Johnathan and gestured for him to put a shirt on. I wanted to say something, but I couldn't find the words. I wanted to leave with Yolanda, but at the same time, I still wanted to be with Johnathan. I wanted him to know that I was still there for him since obviously things were not going to work out between him and Yolanda. Johnathan quickly got dressed and grabbed his keys, but by the time we got outside Yolanda and Aaron were gone.

"I thought you said they were going to be outside." Johnathan stated.

"Well that's what she told me," I said. "She is really upset Johnathan. Why did you have to say something like that, and in front of Aaron? He didn't deserve that. What were you thinking?

"I was just playing around," Johnathan said. "Well they can't be too far. Let's drive around and look for them."

We got in the car and began driving around the neighborhood. There was no sign of either one of them. We drove around for almost 20 minutes.

"Johnathan drive to every bus stop." I said.

There was no sign of Yolanda or Aaron at any bus stop. Johnathan and I decided just to go back to his house and maybe they would show up. As we were driving Johnathan finally commented on what happened. Only I was surprised to hear what he had to say.

"She slapped me," Johnathan said. "I can't believe she slapped me."

"Johnathan what did you expe…" I tried to say before he interrupted my sentence.

"She's fiesty!" he exclaimed. "I like that. Roz, you keep holding out on me. You didn't tell me how pretty she was. And you didn't tell me she was a little firecracker! I hope she is not too mad with me. I really want to get to know her. I think she and I would make a great couple. Don't you think so?'

This was my opportunity to tell Johnathan that Yolanda wasn't interested in him. I could also use this time to tell him how I felt about him. I was so nervous, but I knew it was the right timing.

"Johnathan," I hesitated. "I have something to tell you. But I don't want you to be mad at me."

"I'm not mad at you." he said.

"Not now you're not," I explained. "Johnathan, I told Yolanda that you were interested in her."

He just smiled as he continued driving.

"Roz, I know you did," he said. "You already told me that you and Yolanda are very close. I don't care if she knows. I am almost 32 years old and I should have just been open and honest with her and myself. It's just that I have been rejected so much, I sometimes stall when I should be in hot pursuit. Well, tell me. What did she say?"

I just smiled and looked out the window.

"Let me guess," he said. "She's not looking for a serious relationship now, but she does think I'm cute. So why did she come over this weekend?

"Johnathan, it's just that Yolanda knows that I li..," I gasped as I almost told him my feelings. "Yolanda knows I like hanging out with her, so she came so we could all have fun. And besides, you know that her and Aaron are involved right now. Johnathan, I know there is a girl out there who will love and appreciate you for you. I am almost certain of it."

Johnathan didn't respond to anything that I said. He just looked straight ahead and focused on his driving. When we got to the house, Yolanda and Aaron weren't there. I could tell that Johnathan was not in the best mood, so I volunteered to go home. "Did I tell you that Yolanda walks very fast?" trying to crack a joke about the entire situation. "Look, Johnathan. It's getting late, so you can bring me home now before we get out of the car."

Again, he didn't say anything. He parked the car, got out and went inside. I didn't know if I should go in or start walking home myself. I sat there for a few minutes debating what to do, then Johnathan came out and gestured for me to come inside.

When I came inside Johnathan was just sitting on the sofa staring into space. It was complete silence in the house. Neither one of us said anything for the next fifteen minutes, maybe longer. They only thing I knew to do at this point was to offer him a drink.

"Do you want a beer?" I asked.

"No thank you. I would rather have a glass of wine," he replied.

"Roz why do you drink beers?" he said. "That's so ghetto."

"Ok Mr. Snob," I responded. "I was just trying to be nice. And there is nothing wrong with a nice cold beer. It helps me feel good."

"What else helps you feel good?" Johnathan said with a very strange look on his face.

"Let's see," I thought out loud. "Another nice cold one!"

I was laughing at myself with the help of all the other beers I drank, that I didn't realize that Johnathan was serious.

"What do you mean?" I asked very seriously.

"Can I make you feel good?" he asked. "I don't know about you, but I think we both need something to make us feel good.

I thought I was hearing things. Did Johnathan finally realize that I was that special someone?

"Johnathan, what are you saying." I asked.

"You know what I'm saying." he stated. "It's been a long while since I have been with someone. What about you? If my memory serves me right, it was when Hamp broke your heart several months ago. I can make you feel better than he did."

At that moment Johnathan took me by the hand and led me to the bedroom. I had dreamed about being with Johnathan, but honestly never like this. This was happening very fast. Johnathan wanted to be with me and I wanted to be with him. I stopped thinking and gave in to my flesh!

Johnathan was a gentleman. He noticed there were areas I was unfamiliar with and he guided me. There were areas that I had never experienced, and he took his time. He never said a word. He was in the moment. I was in the moment. There was no turning back. The next hour was more than I could have ever imagined.

Johnathan held me tight before he got dressed. He even gave me a long passionate kiss. I laid there in his bed for almost thirty minutes. I kept praying that I was not dreaming, or worst, trippin' from all those beers. But I knew it was real. I would no longer need to hide my feelings from Johnathan. He obviously felt the same way about me. I was going to tell him on the way home. "Roz, it's getting late," Johnathan said as he called from the other room. "I should probably bring you home."
"Give me a few minutes to get dressed and comb my hair." I said.

The only thoughts that were going through my mind as I got dressed, was how do I tell him, when do I tell him and how much do I tell him. It really didn't matter because we would no doubt be spending a lot more time together. I lived about 10 minutes away from Johnathan, so I knew that I needed to start talking the moment we got in the car. Surprisingly, he started the conversation first.

"Are you ok?" he asked. "You were very quiet, and you still are. Did you like it?"

"Everything is fine," I responded. "Everything was fine. You were a gentleman. Thank you for that. I am just still trying to absorb all of this. If somebody told me that my night would end up like this, I would have called them a liar."

"Well Roz, I know how you feel about me," Johnathan stated. Did he finally put two and two together! This was going to be easier than I thought.

"This doesn't change anything between us," he said. "I know you cherish our friendship as do I. You and I can remain close friends. What happened was just two friends filling a void for each other. I needed to be held and so did you. I would like for this to remain between us. Is that ok with you?"

Johnathan was right about one thing. I did cherish our friendship. In my mind, he was one of the most intelligent people I had ever met. I admired his accomplishments and I was excited about his future. I wanted to remain in his life, even if it meant just as a friend.

He was wrong about filling a void for each other. He just needed somebody to release his manly testosterone into. He said he cherished our relationship, but I didn't believe him. Johnathan was extremely smart and he knew how to use words to his advantage.

I felt so bad about myself that it didn't matter anymore. Who was I fooling? I could never have a serious relationship with somebody like him. I just didn't fit the pretty girl mold. It was just a pattern that had developed with me and guys. All of them use me for their satisfaction. Me, like an idiot, was too blinded by my emotions to even realize it.

Well Johnathan changed all of that for me. I decided to play the game as well. I was going to use the guy before he used me. So, what if I'm not pretty enough to bring home to momma, I didn't want to meet her anyway. I had a very nonchalant attitude that only got worse. If this is what "love" was like, I did not want to have anything to do with it. I just wanted to have fun, no serious commitments unless the guy gave me a definite sign. This was the beginning of a motto I would live by. Of course, I was lonely on the inside, but I never let that appear to anyone. The only values that I had at that point in my life were partying, drinking, and meeting guys. I was willing to do anything to stop that empty feeling.

The next couple of months, he and I filled that "void" for each other behind closed doors. But in the presence of others we were "just friends." He eventually gave up on his quest for Yolanda. Weeks later, he even called and apologized to her for what happened between them. Johnathan and I continued to hang out on the weekends, but Yolanda never joined us again.

He would still invite me to other social affairs. While we were there, he would pass comments about other ladies. Sometimes he would even ask for my advice on how to meet them. Usually at the end of the night before we parted, he would always make a move and I always accepted it. At one point it seemed like I just couldn't say no. He was spending money on me and taking me out to parties and restaurants. Perhaps, deep inside I felt like I owed him something. The one thing I knew how to give was my body.

I never liked myself after being with Johnathan, because it always reminded me that I was not good enough for him, except for one thing. But I was so scared of never experiencing "true" love that I gave into it every time. It seemed like "rebound love" was all that I was ever going to experience

Ladies Night

I knew that my "secret" relationship Johnathan could not go on forever. He was always on the hunt for that special girl and I was just enjoying all the fringe benefits that came my way because he had not found her yet. He had almost turned into a "sugar daddy" for me. I was a broke college student that appreciated somebody dishing out a few extra dollars to help me out.

Johnathan continued to bring me home after class. He would always treat me to lunch or dinner. On the weekends, it was almost understood that we would hook up and do something. At this point in our "friendship," I was getting what I could out of it even though I still had feelings for him. I had transportation without a "car note." I had great meals at some of the best restaurants. And, not to mention, the sex was great! Who needs a commitment? I could go and come as I please, with whomever I pleased. So, that's exactly what I started to do.

Yolanda and I heard about this slamming club, called "Horizons." They had something going on every night of the week. For instance, every Thursday was College Night and if you showed your college ID, you got in free. This was every college students' favorite word "free." It was also the only night Yolanda and I didn't need to use our "fake IDs." You had to be at least 21 years old, with our fake IDs, thanks to an illegal hustle Yolanda and I ran for a while making & selling IDs, Yolanda and I were both 23 years old. Anyway, every Friday Night was Happy Hour, 2 for 1 drinks and finger foods until 7 o'clock. That means chicken drumettes and somebody's sticky jambalaya. But the night of all nights was Sunday. Sunday was Ladies Night, featuring the Male Strippers!!

"Oh yes its Ladies' Night and the feelin's right," I sung to Yolanda. "Hey girl, what time are you coming to pick me up? I want to get there early so we can get a good seat up front."

"Don't worry," she said. "We will be there early so I can see that fine stripper called Mr. Hot Stuff. Girl, I just love it when he comes out in the Fireman Uniform. He gets me hot!"

"No baby," I interrupted. "He ain't got nothing on Irresistible. He is wild. He has no mercy on the girls that are sitting up front. He knows how to make it irresistible."

"You're right," Yolanda agreed. "Ok, I will pick you up at 8:30 tonight. Oh, what are you wearing?"

"Girl, you can't handle this." I said.

"Roz, what are you wearing?" she asked.

"A catsuit!" I screamed. "Why must I be like that, why must I chase the cat? It's nothing but the dog in me!" as I sang a lyric from George Clinton's Atomic Dog. "Girl, I look so good in this outfit I will get chased tonight." I implied. "See ya later and wear something sexy" I exclamed as I rushed off the phone.

I had become obsessed with clothes or the lack thereof. If it wasn't showing off my butt, my waist, or my thighs I probably didn't wear it. Club Horizons was a meeting spot in the "hood" and you had to be ready to compete with the other girls. Yolanda and I spent every waking moment at Club Horizons. Everybody knew us, from the bouncer at the door, the DJ upstairs, the bartenders downstairs, and even the clean-up crew. It was like a second home to us. We went there every night of the week and our main objective was to get drunk and meet guys. In order to do this, you had to look sexy.

One day Yolanda and I went shopping and bought a great pair of pants to wear to the club. Unfortunately, we could not find the right shirt to match. Suddenly we had the crazy idea to create a hot blouse out of a head scarf. I remember going to her house extra early to get dressed if we were wearing our scarves to the club. We both took off our bras and wrapped the scarf around our neck and waist, then viola! I would tie that scarf in the tightest knot ever and she would do the same to me. Then we would do a "test pull" to make sure that it would not make it come off easily.

If we said it was scarf night that meant we were going to Horizon to work our stuff and get whatever guy we wanted. Whenever, it was scarf night, I had to get dressed by Yolanda's house because if my momma saw what I was wearing she would start saying something like, "why buy the cow if you can get the milk for free!" At the time that sounded crazy, but I later realized that I was crazy for rejecting her advice. Even though momma used a lot of old country phrases, she was trying to protect me and teach me to cherish my body, my "temple." But I loved all the attention I would get if I wore provocative clothes. It made me feel like I wasn't an "ugly duckling" anymore.

"Com'on Yolanda, let's sit right here." I said as we pressed our way to the front of the stage.

"I can't wait until the show starts," Yolanda said.

We would religiously go to see the male strippers. I enjoyed it so much that it was like an addiction. I had to be there, no matter what. I would not go to church on Sunday, in order to be well rested to go see Irresistible and the other male dancers. I would even iron the dollar bills that I was going to slip to Irresistible as he worked his stuff for me. My main focus was on Irresistible. I would not have any money for anybody else except Irresistible. I wanted to get to know him and I knew that it would just be a matter of time. I noticed him checking me out a few times, but he never said anything. I just made sure that I was looking good so when he did make a move, I would be ready.

"Ladies I know you have been waiting all night, but the wait is over," said the announcer. "Hold on to your seats and try not to grab too much. But if you can't control yourself, we understand because he's just that I R R E S I S T I B L E!!"

My Story, My Testimony, My Deliverance

I thought I was going to lose my mind every time I heard his named announced. His skin was glistening all over and he was as fine as ever. My eyes were fixated on his every move. I sometimes would escape in my mind and fantasize about being with him. I was in "heat" for this man. All the other guys I had been with, seemed like little boys compared to him. He was 100% man and I thought I was ready for the challenge.

I made sure I gave him a very inviting look whenever he passed me by during his routine; not to mention the places I would put the money, so he could get it. It was almost like I was begging for this man to notice me. As usual another show was over, and I was on cloud nine. Even though he still had not noticed me, I felt like my night was coming soon.

"Girl let's go get something to drink," Yolanda said. "I'm thirsty and I know you should be after all that screaming."

"You were screaming too for that Mr. Fireman." I said while laughing.

"His name is Mr. Hot Stuff." Yolanda stressed.

"Whatever, let's get our drink and find a seat." I said.

We sat there for a while laughing and talking and I noticed a huge crowd of ladies on the other side of the dance floor. It was probably one of the strippers, because all the girls would start flocking around them like they were super stars when they came out of the dressing room. It was Irresistible! I watched him as he made his way to the bar, but he didn't seem to notice me at all. At this time, all the men who were downstairs watching the female strippers were allowed in and the place was getting crowded. Usually at this point, if I have not met him, I would give up until next week. But this night was different. It was my night!

One of the bartenders came over to our table and wanted to know what Yolanda and I were drinking. This happened all the time because we were regulars, so we didn't think anything of it. Also, the bartender had a "thing" for Yolanda, so we got free drinks very often too. We gave him our order and continued to talk and check out the place.

"Who had the gin & 7-up?" It was Irresistible standing at our table with three drinks in his hand.

"I did." said Yolanda.

"So, this rum & coke must be for you?" he asked with a half-smile on his face. "I see y'all come here all the time. What are y'all groupies or something?" he said jokingly. "No seriously, what's your name?" he asked.

"Rosalind," I said with a smile. "But you can call me Roz."

"Yolanda." she said.

"So that's your name, Yolanda." he said.

I was about to scream! This could not be happening again. I was not about to be nobody's fools. I put all those one-dollar bills in his underwear and he was interested in Yolanda. What was going on!!

"My boy, behind the bar, kinda likes you," he said. "He wants you to come and join him at the bar. What do you think?"

I was relieved. I looked at Yolanda to see what she was going to do. When she didn't move fast enough, I decided to step in.

"Girl, free drinks!" I stressed.

It seemed like that was all the convincing she needed, as she quickly got up and left.

"So, can I get a real name?" I asked.

"Mason." he replied.

"I said a real name." as I repeated myself with a confused look on my face.

"Call me weird, but Mason is my last name," he explained. If I told you my first name you would probably laugh. I just like my last name better than my first name.

"So?" I said with curiosity. "Well, what is your first name?"

"That's not important right now," he answered. "But what is important is you and I getting out there on the dance floor, because I love this song.

He just smiled and looked at me, awaiting my response. I was not about to let this moment pass me by. I finished my drink and grab his hand. I loved to dance, and I still do to this very day. The big difference is that I dance to a differentsong. Anyway, Mason was a great dancer. I think it was because he was a stripper. If you wanted to make money and get the ladies attention, you must know how to move your body. And this man knew how to work it. Suddenly, I was the envy of all the other girls in the club as Mason and I danced and played around on the dance floor.

"I'm going to the little boys' rooms," he said. "Why don't you meet me back at the table? I'll be right back."

The strangest thing happened while Mason was in the bathroom. I was sitting at the table finishing my drinks and the bouncer walked over towards me. It was like Yolanda and I practically knew him because he was the first person we saw at the door no matter what day of the week we went to the club. His name was Derrick, but everybody called him Big D. Why? Because he was 6ft, 300 lbs., and solid. He was almost like a big brother to us. More of a brother to Yolanda and an admirer, protector to me. Since our first night coming to the club, Big D was trying to get with me. He was such a sweet person, but not my type at all. He was straight hood and seemed to be involved with some type of mafia type stuff. The dudes he hung with were hard core. Nothing got past him. I guess that's why he was the bouncer. If you even thought about acting stupid, he would bounce yo' a-- right out of there. I always felt a sense of safety because he was always near. Him, Smith and Wesson!

"What's up lil' sis?" he said.

"Hey Big D!" I said cheerfully.

"Where's my hug?", he asked.

I got up and gave him a quick hug.

Then in a very serious voice, he said, "Watch yo' self."

"Big Boy whatcha talkin about?" I asked.

"Ya' boy, Mason," he said. "watch yo' self and be careful. You know I really like you and don't want to see you hurt."

Afterwards Big D walked off and left. He and Mason were friends so why would he tell me that? Was it jealously or genuine concern? I tried not to ponder on it too much because Mason was headed back to the table. It was getting late, so I decided to call it a night.

"Well, Mason it has been a pleasure, but Yolanda and I need to go." I said. "We both have class in the morning."

"I understand," he said. "Here, take my number and call me when you get home to let me know you made it there safely."

So, I did. I took his number and held onto it like it was gold! It made me feel special that he wanted me to know that I made it home safely. I thought that was very considerate. On the way home, Yolanda and I talked about what happened earlier at the club. I was very glad to hear that she was fine while I hung out with Mason. When I walked in the door, I ran upstairs and grabbed the telephone.

"Mason." he answered.

"Hey, it's Roz," I said. "I just made it home safe and sound. What are you doing?

"I'm still at the club thinking about you," he said. "Are you coming tomorrow? Well that's a silly question, because you come every night."

"That's right." I said proudly. "I will be there."

Even though Yolanda and I already went to the club almost every night, the only reason I would go now was to see Mason. I even slacked up on seeing Johnathan. Well at least a little bit.

"Hello," I said, as I answered the phone.

"Hello to you to stranger," he said. "I have been calling you for a few days. Did you get my messages?

It was Johnathan, on the other end of the phone.

"Don't be mad," I said. "I got all your messages, it's just that Yolanda and I had been hanging out at that new club."

"Not Club Horizons?" he asked. "That club is for teeny boppers, drug dealers, and ghetto fabulous people. Where do you fit in?"

"Look," I said. "It's a fun place and I like it. Don't be mad because you're too old to get in."

"Is that where you are going tonight?" he asked.

"Yes, but not until late," I explained. "Yolanda and I usually go around 10 or 11."

"Good, then you can come over here for a little while," he stated. "I can pick you up at 8 o'clock. Tell Yolanda to pick you up at my house for 10:30."

"What if I say no?" I asked.

"You won't." he implied. "We can have a few drinks before you go to the club."

The worst thing about our relationship was that he was right. I knew exactly what Johnathan wanted and why he wanted me to come over. Our relationship was strictly sexual. Forget about all the high society parties and the fancy restaurants, it was all about the sex. Regardless of what I thought, I knew he was using me."

On the other hand, I was doing the same thing just for a different reason. I didn't think I could have anybody that would appreciate me with no strings attached. Most times I just didn't feel worthy to really be loved. I was lonely, and I would try to escape to another world every time I was with him. I realize now that he knew this all the time, but he continued despite my feelings.

I saw him that night before going to the club. The routine was the same. He would have nice music playing in the background and chilled wine sitting on the table. After a few minutes of non-important conversation, he would grab me by the hand and either ask for a hug or lead me to the bedroom. For months, about 90% of the time, I continued to go over whenever he called. I was almost addicted to him and this had become a normal way of living for me.

Beep Beep Beep. That was Yolanda waiting for me outside.

"Roz, why are you going to that club?" Johnathan, asked. "You can stay here, and I'll bring you home later."

"We just had a great time together," I said. "Don't try to put all that sentimental stuff in the picture. How long are we going to do this?"

"I am attracted to you Roz." he said.

"You are physically attracted when nobody else is around." I explained.

Beep Beep BEEEEEP.

"Johnathan, Yolanda is getting impatient." I said.

"Now, what do you mean by that?" he asked. "You know that I have been attracted to you since you were in high school. That has never been a secret to you. It's just that there was a huge age difference between us and I must respect that. You were a minor!"

"Lately Johnathan, you have only been attracted to one thing." I explained.

"Roz what do you want?" Johnathan asked. "I thought we had a good friendship?"

"Johnathan, you would never understand it even if I told you," I said. "I can't keep Yolanda waiting forever. I'll talk to you later." I quickly picked up my bag and headed for the door.

"What in the world took you so long?" Yolanda asked as I closed the car door. "Oh, don't tell me, Johnathan, wanted his own private show before you went to the club?"

"Yolanda, don't start," I said. "You know that I like him, and I would love to have a serious relationship with him, but he doesn't have the same plans."

"Are you ever going to tell him how you feel?" Yolanda asked.

"No, I can't," I said. "I think telling him would ruin the friendship that we have. He wants somebody closer to his age and I don't fit that bill. That's why I am going to enjoy it while it lasts and maybe it will turn around one day. Besides, we do have a good time when we are together so I'm not going to mess that up."

Meanwhile, for the next couple of weeks, Yolanda and I continued to go to Club Horizons. My main concern was to see Mason. I spent most of the nights at the club talking, drinking, and getting to know Mason. On the few nights that we didn't go, I would hook up with Johnathan. I was having fun and living carefree.

Well, another week passed, and it was Saturday again, that meant one more night before Ladies Night at Club Horizons. In order to keep the women hype about it, the strippers always did a 10-minute pre-show on Saturday night. Since I was somewhat seeing Irresistible, Yolanda and I didn't need to get there super early and pray for good seats.

Mason would give the bouncer and all his boys instruction on what to do when we got there. There was always somebody watching out for us. Most nights we didn't need to pay the cover charge, we got free drinks, and Mason made sure that we had front row seats. Mason put on a fantastic pre-show. He was all over me like never before. I was not sure what had gotten into him. But whatever it was I liked it.

"You had fun out there tonight" I said to Mason after his little performance.

"Well I'm glad you enjoyed it," he smiled. "I wanted to make sure you get your money's worth. Look, I'm thirsty. Do you want a drink?"

"Yeah, my usual." I answered.

"I want to get you something different," he said. "You are going to enjoy it. I promise."

I watched Mason walk off towards the bar and smiled in amazement. It was still hard to believe that I was somewhat involved with Mason. This man could probably get whatever he wanted out of me."

"Here, try this," Mason said as he reached me a glass.

"What is it?" I asked.

"Just try it!" he stressed. "You are going to love it!"

I took a little sip and smiled.

"It's pretty good." I said.

"It's a Sex on the Beach." he smiled.

"A what?!" I screamed.

"A Sex on the Beach," he reiterated. "I knew you would like it. Go ahead and finish that and I'll tell my boy to fix you another one. I'll tell him to put some extra cherries in it for you."

The rest of the night Mason and I sat at the table entertaining each other. I showed him this cool trick by tying a knot in a cherry stem. At first, he didn't know what was so spectacular about that, until I did it with my tongue. I have no idea where I learned that, but I had been doing it since basic training. I was always trying to stand out with a guy that I liked and make myself noticeable. It worked the first time for me and I had been doing it ever since. I used that line, "want to know what I can do with my tongue?" This always aroused a guy's curiosity. I did it with Hamp, Spence, Johnathan, so it had to work with Irresistible. "You know Roz we have been hittin' it off really good for the past few weeks," he said. "I don't know how you feel about it, but I want you to come home with me tonight."

JACKPOT!! I had been waiting to hear him say that. I had been lusting after this man for months and I wanted to have him. I was determined to do whatever I had to do to spend the night with him. "Well, you know I came here with Yolanda," I explained. "So, I need to work it out with her. Give me a minute to talk to her. Suddenly, I was so nervous and scared. I was nervous because I wanted to be with Mason, but he was much more experienced than I was. What if I make a fool out of myself? What if he laughs at me? He was definitely on another level than Hamp or Johnathan. He seemed nasty! I was also scared because he was so fine. This man had muscles all over his body. Was he going to hurt my womanhood? Would I be able to handle him?

"Yolanda, girl we gotta talk," I said with excitement. "Irresistible, I mean Mason, wants to spend the night with me! I must be dreaming!"

"How are you going to do that?" she asked.

I just gave her one of those innocent, sad-looking, pitiful faces. "So, I am just supposed to be your personal chaperone?" she asked with an attitude. "Ok, you're living at home with you parents, so what are you going to tell them when you don't show up tomorrow morning?

"Well, we need a ride and you know he doesn't have a car," I explained. "We both need to call home and tell our mom's that we are spending the night by each other's house. I know it will work.

"Well what am I supposed to do while you and he play house?" Yolanda asked.

Just as I was about to think of something to tell Yolanda, Mason walked over to the table and tugged on my arm.

"We can't go to my apartment because my roommate is going to be there," he explained. "But that's ok. We can just go to a hotel.

"Well, I don't think Yolanda is feeling this at all." I said with disappointment.

Mason walked over to the table where Yolanda was sitting and began talking to her. He was so smooth, I knew he would be able to convince her. Just like I predicted, he did. Once he finished talking to her, he walked off smiling.

"So, it's all good?" I asked. "I saw you and Mason in a deep conversation over here.

"Yeah, he agreed to pay for my hotel room and give me gas money." she smiled.

I was floating on a cloud for the rest of that night. Finally, what I had been dreaming about for the past month or two was about to become a reality. After that night, I knew I was going to be the envy of all the women in the place. I just wanted to be able to handle it and not look like an amateur. I told Yolanda about my nervousness and she could not give me any advice other than to stop and get some Vaseline!

As we were getting ready to leave the club, Yolanda and I walked down the street to a payphone to call each other's mom. Neither one of them questioned Yolanda or me. I ask myself now the question, why? It was already 1 o'clock in the morning and we were not even close to coming home. But then, we call and say we are spending the night over at our friend's house and nobody asks why? Maybe they were too caught up in their own affairs to be bothered? Perhaps they both knew we were lying but felt hopeless.

As Yolanda and I were walking back to the club, Big Boy was standing outside staring at me. I wanted to ask him what he meant about that comment he made the other night, but I decided that I didn't want anything to ruin my night with Mason. At that point, what I didn't know could not hurt me.

Mason was standing outside waiting on us. He had this real serious look on his face. I saw him talking to a couple of guys at the door and nodding his head towards us. Then I saw all of them "dapping" him up like he was the man, everybody except for Big Boy. I wonder what his actual words were. If I had to take a guess, it wasn't "this is the kind of girl you take home to momma." "Hey bae, are you ready?" he asked with a serious look in his eyes.

I just nodded my head. I think I was too excited to speak, and if I said something I would probably sound like a teenage girl with the giggles. When I think back, I was a teenager. As we walked to the car, I noticed somebody following us. He didn't say a word, but he was checking Yolanda out.

"Mason, who is that guy?" I asked with concern. "He's following us."

"Oh, that's Robert," he said calmly. "He is coming with us."

"What do you mean he is coming with us?" I asked.

109

"Well, I didn't want Yolanda to be by herself," he explained. "He's cool. Don't worry about it. They will have their room, and we'll have ours."

I didn't want to tell Yolanda, so I stopped walking and pulled Mason aside to talk.

"I'm worried about Yolanda," I stressed. "You didn't tell her that somebody else was going to be in the room with her. She doesn't even know this man. You better go over there and tell her because I'm not."

Mason went over to the car and introduced Yolanda to Robert. He just explained to Yolanda that this was his boy and he really needed a ride home. Yolanda agreed, because she knew Mason was giving her gas money. It's just that he didn't explain to Yolanda it would be in the morning.

"Ok Mason, where are we going?" Yolanda asked.

"It's on the west bank," he said. "Just head towards the bridge and I'll give you directions from there."

It didn't take a long time at all to get there. Mason seemed to know exactly where he was going. Apparently, this was not his first time going to this hotel. It was at this moment also, I think Yolanda realized that she was going to have an extra guest in her boudoir. We parked the car in front of the door and left the motor running while Mason and Robert went inside to get our hotel rooms.

I apologize did I say hotel? A hotel is a place where there is valet parking, bellmen outside to greet you, and beautiful landscaping. We were at a Motel 6 and it was horrible! The bulbs were out on the sign so it actually read "Mo el 6." There were no lights outside, which caused the place to look abandoned. I was scared somebody was going to break into the car. That's bad because Yolanda didn't have a Benz, she had a 1979 hatchback! There should have been no reason for that unnecessary stress. I had enough on my mind with trying to figure out how to handle this man!

"Yolanda, please don't be mad about Robert," I said. "I didn't know this was part of the plan. It's just that I really want to be with Mason and I know he wants to be with me. He was just trying to make you enjoy your night as well."

"I am going in that room and I am going to sleep," she explained. "He better not try anything, because I am not in the mood for foolishness. Don't worry about me. You better worry about yourself and Mason. He's a big guy!!"

"Yolanda, I can't believe that I'm here with Mason." I said. "I am a little nervous, but I after tonight I will be alright!"

Mason and Robert came back to the car with big smiles on their faces. Mason wasn't concerned about anything else at this moment except getting up to that room. I gave Yolanda my room number and told her to give me a call if she needed me for anything. Suddenly, I was more nervous for Yolanda than myself. She just met Robert for the very first time in her life, at least I knew Mason. It had been at least 10 or 12 weeks of us talking and seeing each other at the club. In my opinion, 2 weeks was a long time and this man was fine."

"Roz, I'll be right back," Mason said as he went in to the bathroom. "Go ahead and get comfortable.

I didn't know what "get comfortable" meant. I tried to relax, but it was difficult. Mason came out of the bathroom wearing nothing but his spandex underwear. I was still sitting on the edge of the bed looking nervous.

"What's the matter baby? He asked in amazement. "You're still dressed."

"Look, Mason, I need to tell you something," I hesitated. "You will probably be surprised, but I'm not that experienced as you. I don't want you to laugh at me."

"Roz, everything will be fine," he assured me. "You don't need to worry. Take off your clothes and I'll grab some beers I have in my bag. It will help you relax."

Mason reached me a beer, but before I could really enjoy it, he started kissing and rubbing me all over. I just became lost in his touch. I forgot all about everything and decided to enjoy the moment, well almost everything.

"Mason, do you have a condom?" I asked.

"I don't like wearing condoms," he said. "I can't feel anything when I wear it. Don't worry, it's ok."

"No, seriously Mason," I explained. "You need to wear one."

"They never fit me right," he said. "Besides, I don't know if I have one in my bag. Don't you have some in your purse?"

"No, why would I have condoms in my purse?" I said. Anyway, I'll just call Yolanda and we can go to the store to buy some." I said.

As I reached for the phone, Mason got up and clicked on the night lamp. He never said a word, instead he walked over to grab his bag and pulled out his wallet. Not only did he have one condom, he had several in his wallet. He came back to the bedside and gave me a sly grin.

"You sure you want me to wear this?" he asked.

"Please?" I asked with an innocent look on my face.

Mason didn't look thrilled at all, but he did it for me anyway. He acted like he was having difficulty getting it to fit properly, but I never said a word. His attitude had changed a little in the last few minutes and I was trying not let it kill the mood. I was also busy trying to figure out why he thought I should have condoms in my purse. What kind of girl did he think I was? Obviously, he didn't think too highly of me if he asked that question.

However, it was nobody's fault but my own. I made the decision to be there with him. All I wanted to do was be in his arms. I had fantasized about Mason ever since I saw him dance across that floor. He was hot, and, in my mind, I had to be with him. He came back to the bed and turned the lights off.

The next hour or so was interesting. Mason totally took charge of everything and turned me into a circus acrobat. As I assumed, he was more experienced than me. I wanted to make a good impression on him, so I followed his every move and did whatever he asked.

"Roz, can I take it off?" he whispered.

I had to snap out of wonderland to concentrate on what he was asking.

"Can I take it off?" he said.

"I thought you said you were going to wear it? I answered.

"What's the matter?"

"Com'on baby just for a few minutes," he whined. "I can't feel it."

For a brief moment, I could remember my momma telling me, "Roz, don't you come home with no baby or I'm gonna send yo' butt to the country." I can't get pregnant.

"Mason, just leave it on please." I stated.

For the next few minutes, he just kept trying to convince me that he couldn't feel it all the way, but I ignored it. I just didn't want to be nineteen with a baby on the way. I could tell he wasn't giving up that easily, because he continued to say please for a while. Every time he asked, he would attempt to take it off and I was saying no and moving his hand. This went on for at least ten minutes. It became a struggle, as he grabbed and pulled, and I grabbed and pulled. Whenever I tried to say something, he would shove his tongue down my throat. All of a sudden, he stopped asking. He completely stopped. Everything was fine, and Mason was back in his groove.

A few hours later while lying in the bed, I glanced over at Mason and I wanted to scream with excitement. I couldn't believe I was there with him. Our relationship had advanced to another level and I was definitely going to be the envy of every woman at the club. I spent the rest of the night laying in his arms until morning.

Ring...Ring...Ring...

"Hello...yeah, hold on." Mason said as he reached me the telephone.

"Hey girl," I said. "Are you okay?"

"I'm fine," Yolanda said assuredly. "The question is, how are you? I see that you survived through the night. How was it?! Do you feel okay?"

I really couldn't talk openly, because Mason was lying in the bed right beside me.

"Yeah, we can go get something to eat," I said to give her a clue that I couldn't talk. "I'll call you after we get dressed."

"Uh Oh," Yolanda said and giggled. "Call me back."

I hung the phone up and laid back down next to Mason. I didn't want this night, morning, nothing to end. As I was thinking about our night together, Mason begin to wake up.

"Good Morning," he said in a deep voice. "What did ya' girl want?

"Oh, she's just hungry." I said.

"She's hungry?" he asked with a grin. "Did she work up an appetite last night?"

"Yeah, from her snoring." I replied sarcastically. "You're the one who should be tired, from all of your 'ringmaster tricks.'"

Mason just laughed and said, "You didn't stop me!" Then he took the phone off the hook and round two had begun.

"Mason, what you are doing?" I asked. "Do you have …

"I just want to feel it one more time before we leave," he said. "It's ok, trust me."

We fooled around for the next 15 minutes until, we were both too caught up to stop. I tried to make him take it out before he climaxed, but it didn't happen.

"Look, I'm going to take a shower." he said as he gave me a kiss. The minute he closed the door I picked up the phone and waited until I heard the water before I called Yolanda.

"GIRL, GIRL, GIRL…it was on!" I exclaimed. "Last night and a few minutes ago!"

"So, you finally got what you wanted." she asked.

"It was more than what I asked for." I explained. "You know how it is when you want something, and I had to have this man."

"So, you feel ok?" she hinted. "You know…feel ok?"

"I feel fine." I said reassuring her. "It is all a myth, lies all lies."

"WHAT!!!" she screamed. "All those muscles…"

"You know the saying, "big things come in small packages?" I asked. "Well let's say that it's a shame to have something so small in a big ole 'package! It's a waste of room. Look, I gotta go I just heard him turn the shower off. We'll be ready to leave in about 45 minutes."

Mason walked out of the bathroom laughing.

"You know what I wanted to tell you about last night?" he asked. "We had a little accident."

"Accident?" I asked with curiosity. "What are you talking about?

As I tried to figure out what was going on, Mason reached on the floor besides the bed and picked up the used condom and placed his finger straight through it. I was so clueless and "green" that I didn't know what I was looking at.

"It bust." he said with a grin.

"What do you mean it bust?" I asked.

I was too embarrassed to tell him I didn't know that could happen, therefore I just decided to ask him how.

"How?" I asked.

"Well, I told you they don't fit me right," he explained. "I guess I'm just too big for them. I thought you knew."

Right then and there, I knew that was his imagination and his "big ego" talking because he and I knew that wasn't the truth. But I digress.

"How would I have known?" I asked in amazement.

"It feels different," he said. "Once that happened, I was able to get into the groove."

Immediately, my mind flashed back to last night when we both were debating whether he could take off the condom or not. It was more of a struggle once I really thought about it. He was trying to take it off and go back in, while I was fighting with him to stop. I was so upset.

117

"Mason, that's not good," I said. "What if something happens?
"Something like what?" he asked sarcastically. "You mean, like getting pregnant. Girl, you trippin'. You'll be fine."
I was very frustrated with his attitude. "I'll be right back," I said. "I need to go shower. I think Yolanda wants to leave soon."

Obviously, I just said that, so I could get myself together in private. I jumped into the shower and tried to relax, but questions began to flood my mind. How could he do that? He knew that I was serious when I said, "no don't take it off" and since it ripped, he should have cared enough about me to stop and get another one. I really think it ripped because of all the pulling. Still today something inside of me said "it was not an accident." Did he really care? Suddenly, I became sick to my stomach thinking, what if I get pregnant? Mason had ejaculated inside of me. I had never let that happen before. I knew it was possible for an unwanted pregnancy when you don't protect yourself. He was so nonchalant about it, but it was a real factor for me. I didn't want to seem like a frantic little girl, so I decided to "be cool" and wait a few weeks to see what happened. I really liked Mason and I didn't want anything to come between us.

Soon after, we checked out of the motel and headed home. I didn't want to leave Mason, but knowing I was going to see him that night at the club made it better. First, we dropped off Robert at his apartment. Somehow, I knew this would be the first stop Yolanda was going to make. As, we drove to Mason's apartment,

I paid close attention to all the turns and streets because in my mind I was planning on seeing him again.

"Well, this is my stop." he said. "Thanks Yolanda."

"Yeah, Yeah, get out." she said jokingly.

I leaned in towards him for a kiss good-bye, as the car stopped.

"I'll call you later." I said.

"I'll see you tonight." he said as he walked off.

Yolanda and I both waited until we were around the corner before we let out a great big SCREAM! I was excited, and Yolanda was excited for me! I had slept with Mr. Irresistible. I spent the night in his arms and now I was above the rest of the women at the club. "I can't wait until I get to the club tonight to see him," I sighed. I felt like I was on cloud nine.

"So, you did have a good time?" Yolanda asked.

"Yeah, it was great." I said. "But, guess what? He didn't want to wear a condom. I had to beg him to do it and then after having it on for less than 10 minutes, he wanted to take it off because he couldn't feel it."

"Well it does feel different," she said. "Sometimes Aaron and I use them and sometimes we don't. But you didn't let him take it off?"

"No, but he tried to pull it off," I explained.

"That's good," Yolanda said with relief. "Maybe later...

I interrupted. "No, not good," I said. "it ripped. I have no idea, but he knew because he told me this morning."

"How do you know for sure?" she asked.

119

"He showed it to me," I said. "and trust me, he's not lying. He was trying to pull it off, and I was trying to put I back in. We both were going back and forth last night so that's probably when it happened. He said it with a smile on his face this morning. He was ok, because he said once that happened, he was able to get into his groove."

"Did he...you know...inside of you?" she hesitated.

"Yup." I said.

"It's ok," Yolanda said. "When is your period coming?

Shaking my head in disbelief I said, "Around the 19th."

"So, let's not panic," she said. "We'll wait until the 30th and then worry if we need to. No matter what, you're not in this by yourself."

The closer we got to my house, I got nervous. I knew that I lied about sleeping over by Yolanda's house and even though they bought the lie, I was feeling convicted. But since my mind was not on pleasing my parents, I knew deep down that I would do it again. I was satisfying my flesh. I felt like I was old enough to do what I wanted to do.

It felt good being with Mason last night. Every time I was with Johnathan it felt good, for the moment. Even when I thought back to all the changes I went through to be with Hamp before I left base, it felt good having been with him. Yeah, I had some heartache with Hamp and Anthony, but Mason was going to be different. This turned out to be 100% true. What I experienced with Mason was life changing.

My Story, My Testimony, My Deliverance

I laid around the house for the rest of the afternoon thinking about my night with Mason and how I loved being with him. Unfortunately, every time I called his apartment to tell him what a good time I had, he never answered the phone. I continued to call for hours and still no answer. But what made it worst, is that he never called me.

Well, it was Saturday afternoon, and this was usually around the time that Yolanda and I start planning our outfits for Ladies Night at the club.

"Hey girl, whatcha doing?" Yolanda said on the other end of the phone.

"Nothing." I responded.

"Nothing?" she asked. "What's wrong with you? You were supposed to call me 30 minutes ago, so we could decide what we're wearing tonight. Wait a minute. You're not still worried about that condom ripping, are you? Roz, please forget about it. Everything will be ok. Let's just wait a few weeks and then if we need to, we'll deal with it then. But tonight, it's Ladies Night and if I'm not mistaken you are now Mrs. Irresistible! When Yolanda said that, it made something on the inside of me rise. I was his woman and he was my man!

"Well, I was a little upset, because he's not answering his phone. I have been calling him all day, but it's cool."

I really didn't want to tell Yolanda that I wasn't feeling too hot. The last few times I was with Johnathan, I was feeling this way

121

and now the same feeling happened with Mason. It was probably nothing.

"Girl, that man is probably wore out!" she screamed. "Leave him alone. You'll see him tonight right after the show. Now get out yo' halter and your black mini and don't forget the G-string! I'll pick you up around 9 o'clock."

Yolanda was right. Tonight, was going to be different from all the other nights, because I was officially attached to Mason. I began pulling myself out of that rut and started getting ready.

When we got to the club, Big Boy was the first person we saw. He let us in with no questions asked, but I had a strange feeling that he wanted to ask me about Mason and me. But I think he knew the answer already. Yes, I left with Mason last night and there was no turning back. I just quickly went inside to get a drink and grab a good seat. It was time.

The smoke screen filled the club and the strobe lights were flashing. The announcer came out and started pumping up the crowd. Out of all 4 strippers, Mason was the last one. I was so ready to see him.

"Ladies, tonight we saved the best for last!" the announcer said. "Now get yo' bills out and let me hear you scream for I R R E S I S T I B L E!!"

I tried to scream my head off because I wanted to let him know that I was in the house. Mason was on fire as usual. He danced on the floor, the counter top, and the bar stools. When he passed by Yolanda and me, I just caressed his cheek gently to give him a hint that I wanted more tonight. I forgot all about the fact that I put myself at risk of being a mom.

At the time I was not sure what was happening to me. I just wanted to drink, party, and have sex. It was fun. I had been chained up for so long and now that I had a taste of freedom, I was making up for lost time. I felt like I owed it to myself. Not fully understanding, I just kept giving in to my flesh and kept sinking deeper and deeper into sin. This seemed normal to me.

Even though I was raised in the church, sang in the youth choir, and gave my determination every third Sunday, with a folded piece of tissue shaped into the perfect triangle on top of my head, I thought it was fine to do what I wanted because I was young and deserved to have fun. Who in the world cared what I did with my life? It was my life.

The show ended, and as usual, all the women were flocked around the door waiting for the dancers to come out. I kept trying to get a glimpse of Mason, so I could show him where we were sitting. "Do you see Mason, Yolanda?" It was so crowded in the club tonight, I never saw him come out of the dressing room. "He's probably over there somewhere," she replied. "You better go get your man."

I decided to take her advice, so I could find Mason and ask him if he wanted to leave. Before I made it over to the other side of the club, Big Boy was headed my way.

"Hey lil' sis," he said. "Where you off to in such a hurry?"

"I was looking for Mason," I said. "Is he downstairs?"

"Well, he was downstairs," Big Boy said sarcastically. "but he left."

I had this puzzled look on my face. "What do you mean he left. Are you sure?"

"Mason comes and goes," he said. "He'll be back."

Big Boy walked off before I got a chance to ask him about the comment, he made the other night. He seemed confident that Mason was coming back, so I didn't worry.

"Where's Mason," Yolanda asked.

"Big Boy said he left, but he'll be right back." I said trying not to worry.

There were several guys that came over to the table who wanted to dance, or buy me a drink, but out of my obligation to Mason, I turned everybody down. If I did dance, I danced alone. I would be on the dance floor by myself with a drink in one hand to make sure everybody knew I was having fun all by myself. After an hour, finally, Mason appeared. I was excited to see him. All I wanted to do was give him a big hug.

"Hey, you," I said as if he was a long-lost friend that I just bumped into. "I called you earlier today. Are you alright?"

"Yeah," he said. "Look, I'm on the clock tonight so I can't sit around all night talking. "If you want a drink, let them know I got it. I'll be back to check on you later."

I felt like a little red corvette just passed me by going 100 mph! That was the most conversation I had with Mason the entire night. He worked full-time at the club, as well as the other strippers, as a bartender or as a bouncer. Usually he still had time to sit for a while and talk, but he didn't talk to me at all. He spent half of the night walking around playing "security chief" and the other half talking to another female on the other side of the club. There were several times, Mason walked right passed me and acted as if he didn't even know me. We just spent the night together less than a full 24 hours ago and he was ignoring me.

It was obvious that he knew that woman, who was much older than him. She looked like she was in her mid-40s. She was wearing a glitter dress, with costume jewelry. I don't even know why she was at the club. Perhaps it was girl's night out for her and a few friends, because she was truly out of her league, or was she?

At that point I was upset and embarrassed. Everybody at the club knew that Mason and I left with each other last night. They all knew that we did not go to catch a late movie. I looked like a fool because he was with this other woman. Who in the hell was she? I thought Mason cared about me. Just then, I noticed Mason get up from the table and started making his way over to my side of the club.

I pretended not to notice him, but as soon as he got close, I jumped up from my seat. "Mason can I talk to you for a minute?" I asked. "What the hell is going on? Who is that lady you're talking to?"

I had attitude all over the place. I demanded an answer from Mason. We were boyfriend and girlfriend, right? So, I had a right to know. Mason didn't talk right away. Instead, he just looked at me as if I were crazy for questioning him. He took one step and got directly in my face and began to talk through his teeth, as if he was pissed off.

"Who the hell do you think you are?" he said. "You don't ever talk to me like that. Now you get your ass home and I will call you later. Alright?"

I stood there frozen solid as Mason walked off continuing to make his rounds. He was a different person, definitely not the man I spent the night with less than 24 hours ago. The only reason I went to the club was to see Mason, and since he was obviously preoccupied, I decided to leave. I was scared, but it did sound good for a minute. As I was saying, I didn't see Yolanda anywhere, so that meant I had to stay there longer watching him talk to this other lady. I wanted to go over there and cuss her ass out! But that would have started a big mess. Finally, I saw Yolanda on the dance floor and I motioned for her to come over. Yolanda never came off the dance floor, so I had to go to her.

"Look, I'm ready to go." I said firmly.

"Girl I'm just getting started," she said shaking her groove thang. "What's wrong?" You haven't found yo' man yet?"

"Yeah, I found him," I hesitated. "it's just that I don't like who I found with him. He's been over there talking to the same woman all night. We barely talked to each other."

"Well who is she?" asked Yolanda.

Embarrassment was all over me. "He won't say," I said in a low voice. "he told me to leave."

"He said what?" screamed Yolanda. "He can't tell you what to do."

"Yolanda it's okay," I said trying to calm her down. "I want to leave."

I went downstairs to wait for Yolanda and have a moment to myself. I also decided to let two good friends, Jack & Coke join me. As I was sitting at the table trying to figure out what happened, Big Boy walked up and took a seat.

"I take it you saw Mason upstairs." Big Boy said. Why don't you and yo girl call it a night?"

"Why? So, Mason can do his dirt in the open and not in the back-corner upstairs?" I replied. "Who is she?"

"Look lil' sis," Big Boy said in a soothing voice. "The problem is not who she is, but who Mason is. I tried to give you a clue the other night. Mason is my boy, but he has a reputation for being a lady's man."

"Well he told me that he wasn't involved with anyone," I said. "and I believed him."

"Mason is NOT involved with ANY ONE. He is involved with EVERY ONE. He loves women, especially older women who are financially stable. See upstairs, that's probably his rent money, so he can't spend time with anyone else tonight."

"Big Boy, I have been coming to this club for a while and I have watched Mason," I explained. "He doesn't look like that type of person at all."

"Now, hasn't yo' momma ever told you that looks can be deceiving?" he said. "Look, I said before and I'm saying it again, watch yo' self with Mason."

Despite the warning signs from Big Boy, I continued to be involved with Mason. It had gotten to the point that I accepted Mason and all the other women that he was messing with. Within the next few weeks, I realized that I was one of at least four, five, or six women he was giving private shows to at night. I could always tell if it was my night to be with Mason because the minute, I made eye contact with him, he smiled and immediately came over to give me a kiss. If it wasn't my night, he would not make eye contact and he would stay on the opposite side of the club. He would pass by and act like he didn't even know my name. The worst part is that I accepted his actions. I let him walk over me like I was nothing. I let Mason use me repeatedly. The nights he didn't want to be bothered with me, I hooked up with Johnathan. This cycle went on for a few months. I was having fun with Mason and Johnathan, but at the same time just desiring to be in a relationship. I wanted somebody to care. I was so determined to find that right person, I was willing to do anything.

One night when I was leaving the club around 2 am, there was this guy that I had been flirting with all night. He was a good-looking brother. I really wanted to get back at Mason for acting as if I was his puppet. So, when he approached me, I did not refuse his conversation.

"Don't I know you from somewhere?" he said. "you look very familiar."

"I don't think so, but we can get to know each other?" I said.

"My name is Tony" he said. "I was checking you out earlier, but first I wanted to make sure you weren't here with yo' man or nothing."

"No man or boyfriend" I replied. "Just having fun."

Tony and I talked in the parking lot for almost an hour. We appeared to have a lot in common. He was around my age. He had never been in any real kind of trouble. He liked having fun. What more did I need to know? When I told Mason that I met somebody close to my age, he was glad. But it didn't stop either one of us from kicking it from time to time.

It had only been about three weeks of Tony and I talking on the phone occasionally when he invited me over to his house. I was excited about seeing somebody different, somebody new. I was acting like it was my first date or something. We weren't doing anything spectacular. Tony lived with his dad and every Sunday during football season they watched the game. So, I was going over to hang out and watch the game. As I pulled into his driveway, I began to sweat.

"Hey Tony," I said with a huge grin. "what's up?"

"Nothing much baby girl." he replied. "I couldn't wait til you got here.I mean, I been thinking' bout you all day," he said. "Well let's go in so you can meet my pops."

Tony was so excited. He grabbed my hand and quickly led me inside.

"Hey pops, this is my girl Rosalind." Tony said with his chest puffed out. "We been kickin' it for a while now."

"Hello," I said. "Nice to meet you."

"Hey baby," he responded. "Come on in and have a seat. You're just in time for the game."

Now I really wasn't interested in the game, but I forced myself to get through it. I forced myself to get through the next three games!! Tony and his dad were fanatics. They watched game, after game, after game, drinking beer and eating popcorn. I sat and sat and sat pretending to be interested in each field goal, touch down, and interception. Even though Tony was a fanatic, every commercial or halftime he was very affectionate and all into me. He was giving me either gentle kisses or leg messages. At first, I was a little uncomfortable because his dad was right there on the other couch, but it didn't bother Pops one bit. Tony and his dad acted more like roommates more than father and son. So, his dad let Tony do his thang. As the time passed by, eventually Tony's dad was calling it a night.

"Alright baby," Pop's said. "I'll see y'all later."

The minute his dad shut his bedroom door, Tony and I were all over each other. This went on for about an hour. I already knew where this was leading. At least I thought I knew where it was leading me. The most difficult question I had at this time was are we using the sofa or the bed. I wasn't thinking about protection or anything. Again, I was just so caught up in the pleasure of sin for a moment.

"Wait," Tony said. "I can't get comfortable." "Let's go in my room so we can take our time."

"Ok," I said. "but is Pop's cool with this?"

Tony looked at me as if I was trying to tell a real funny joke. Which looking back on that night, the look he gave me should have been a sure sign that I wasn't the first girl going to his room to get more "comfortable."

"Pop knows the deal." he said. "besides his girl was here last night and I didn't bother them one bit. Look, we're wasting time."

So, once I realized it was cool with everybody, I stopped asking questions and followed Tony to his room.

This night was unlike any other night I have ever had. It had nothing to do with Tony or his performance however, it had everything to do with me. As Tony and I were too far gone to turn around, I began to have a strange feeling in my body. The music was right, the lights were right, the place was right, but I wasn't right. I had that strange feeling again that I experienced a few times after being with Johnathan and Mason. The real strange thing is that I would usually get that feeling a day or two after, but this time I was experiencing that uncomfortable, tingling sensation right in the heat of the moment. This continued until the early morning hours. I tried to stay focused on the moment, however, the tingling sensation, now a little painful was overriding that moment. As I kissed Tony goodbye the next day, I couldn't wait to see him again. However, little did I know that was my first and last night being with Tony.

FIVE

The next few days after being with Tony were the worse. I was feeling awful. My body was achy all over and there was a tingling sensation that was ripping through my thighs and lower back like crazy! I was even swollen in certain areas around my thighs. I didn't go to any of my classes, missed two days of work, and I wasn't thinking about the club. All I wanted to do was lay in the bed and rest. Surely after a few days in bed and two aspirin, I should be feeling much better. Then Wednesday morning it grew into the worse pain I ever felt in my life!

I decided to get up and end the tiresome fight with the pillow. I hadn't gotten any sleep for the past few days. The short trip from the bed to the bathroom was very difficult because now the walking caused me to be in great pain. By the time I made it to the bathroom, I was in tears. There was such a burning. I wanted to scream during my normal morning routine. Did Freddie Kreuger slice me up during the middle of the night? I felt like there were cuts and wounds in the strangest places. I was so scared. Immediately I grabbed the phone to call Yolanda.

"Hey Yo" I whispered. "Wake up! I need to talk to you."

"What's the matter?" Yolanda asked.

"Girl, I don't feel good." I said. "I can't use the bathroom!"

"Whatcha mean you can't use the bathroom?" Yolanda asked in a concerned voice. "That's crazy."

"It's burning too bad!" I cried. "I think something is wrong. There's also this nasty discharge."

"This just started this morning?" Yolanda said in a condescending voice.

'Yes, this just started!" I yelled. "What difference does it make?" The problem is that it's happening now. I'm in pain and I need your advice."

"Ok, calm down" she said. "You need to go to the doctor."

"Now you know I don't have a doctor" I said.

"Well not like a 'doctor' doctor'" she said. "I mean like a clinic doctor. My mom had a friend that used to work at a clinic specifically for girls. You never heard of it?"

"No" I said. "What is the name of it?"

"I'm not too sure, but I think it's something like parenthood clinic?" she said reluctantly. "Just go through the phone book, look under clinics, and see what you find."

"Alright" I sighed. "I'll let you know what I find."

I wanted to move at lightning speed, however the pain in my thighs and between my legs would not allow it. I decided to take a quick shower and freshen up a bit before I went downstairs by the rest of the family. Unfortunately, nothing at this point was quick. I was in so much pain, even the water from the shower was hurting. What in the world was going on?! What was happening? Everything was fine a few days ago.

I thought I would never make it down all those stairs, but finally I made it. I moved as fast as I could and grabbed the yellow pages and at the same time praying that my mom didn't ask what I was looking for. It took me a while to sit down and get comfortable because as I was in such severe pain. But finally, I bared through it and found a clinic not too far from my house. I jotted the number down and then slowly went back upstairs to my room for some privacy.

"Hello, Family Planning," said the voice on the other end of the phone. "Can you hold please?"

"Yes, "I replied, but my inside was screaming NOOOOOOOO!

"This is Kim, how can I help you?" the receptionist asked.

"Umm, I think I need to see a doctor," I mumbled, "I'm not feeling too well."

"What do you mean, you're not feeling well?" she asked.

"Well, it is hard for me to use the bathroom," I whispered, "it's burning too bad!"

The nurse Kim was very patient. It was obvious that she had experience in what she was doing. I was nervous and embarrassed, but she never made me feel that way. For the next 5 minutes or so, she proceeded to ask several questions like name, address, number etc. etc.

"Ok Rosalind," she said in a calm voice, "The doctor can see you next Friday and 11am."

I thought I was going to drop the phone! That was 7 days away.

"Next Friday," I asked. "Ms. Kim, I don't think I can wait until next Friday. I am in pain." "Is there anything sooner?" I said desperately?

"I'm sorry baby, but we are booked until then." she explained.

The next week was horrible for me! Everything was painful. Sitting was painful. Walking was painful. Using the bathroom was ridiculously painful! I had to pour warm water between my legs in order to use the bathroom without crying! There was no relief AT ALL!! What was going on? My body was aching all over especially between my legs. I was scared. The only person I could talk to was Yolanda and she really didn't understand what I was going through. She tried, but it wasn't her feeling my pain.

One morning I went to the bathroom and decided to play doctor myself. I took a small compact mirror and examined myself. I could feel that something was wrong, but now I wanted to see for myself. I put the mirror in a position that would show me something and I was in shock! The discharge was nasty. I saw several open sores with this white puss on the inside. Then I also felt several small bumps. Without a big enough mirror, I couldn't see the bumps to clearly, but they were tiny white clusters. Please Lord, let 11 o'clock Friday come soon.

"Hey girl, are you ready?" Yolanda asked.

"I have been up and ready since 9 o'clock this morning." I said.

"Yo, I'm so glad today is Friday. Girl this had been a week. You just don't know what I have been going through."

"Well, everything is gonna be fine," Yolanda said, "I'm certain of it."

After I hung up with Yolanda, I decided to start making my way downstairs. It literally was taking me almost 5 minutes to walk down 10 stairs. But all I could think about was the fact that this was all going to be over by noon. I finally made it downstairs and to the car. I was glad my mom didn't ask where I was going. She was busy in the kitchen fixing breakfast, so she can eat and watch Young & the Restless for 11 o'clock. So, I just spoke and got out of the house as fast as I could. I was also glad that by this time I had an inexpensive car of my own. I called her two-toned Bertha. She was a point car, meaning it got me from point A to point B, rattling and all.

The clinic wasn't far. I made it there and found a parking spot in about 20 minutes. Now even though it was the Friday I had been waiting for, I still hesitated about getting out of the car. You see, after I made the appointment, I did a little research on Family Planning. This place was a family planning clinic for girls. It serviced girls that were sexually active and those that were pregnant. You didn't even have to pay a dime for anything. If you were in school, it was a free service.

137

I just didn't want anybody to see me, so I had to get it together before I went it. I had been on this street hundreds of times and never noticed the clinic. It was right down the street from the Laundromat we went to, the drugstore we were always in, and the best fried chicken place in town that we ate at all the time. Some of you might know the name, in the cartoons his girlfriend's name was Olive Oil. Johnathan even lived 5 minutes away. I couldn't believe it. Anyway, after playing FBI I scoped the streets good, then made a mad dash inside the clinic.

"Hi, my name is Rosalind," I said reluctantly, "I have an 11 o'clock appointment.

"Ok, sign in," the person said, "I need you to complete this paperwork and have a seat until the doctor calls you."

It seemed like I waited for the longest time, but it was only about 10 minutes. I was just ready to put this behind me and move on!

"Rosalind?" the nurse asked.

I wanted to jump up and run like I was carrying the winning touchdown on Super Bowl Sunday, but instead I rose slowly and followed the nurse to the other room.

"Ok Rosalind, what brings you in to see the doctor today?" asked the nurse.

'Well," I said nervously, "I just have not been feeling well."

I proceeded to tell the nurse what's been going on. I even told her what I saw the other day in the bathroom with my compact mirror. She listened closely and wrote everything down in my chart.

"Rosalind, I need you to get undressed from waist-down, drape yourself, and wait for the doctor." she explained.

The doctor came shortly after and was very nice. I was very surprised because the doctor was a man. I had never been to a doctor other than my childhood pediatrician and that was a woman. So, I was a little embarrassed but what could I do? I needed to be examined. The doctor looked at the notes the nurse wrote down and asked me a few questions. I answered them as honestly as I could, so he could make it all better. The doctor told me slide up on the table and place my feet in the strangest things. He told me to take a deep breath and try to relax.

The exam took a little while. I lot of feeling, touching, rubbing with Q-tips, and uncomfortable cold instruments, but finally the worst was over. He told me to get dressed and he would come back to talk to me in a few minutes. The pain was intensified since he examined me, so my movements were even slower. Knock knock, then the door opened.

"Ok Rosalind," the doctor said, "I had a chance to look under the microscope and reviews the slides." "The reason why you have been in so much pain is because you have contracted an S.T.D.," he said.

I was so ignorant, because I had no idea what he was talking about. "What is that?" I asked.

"Rosalind STDs are Sexually Transmitted Diseases," he explained, "you can contract an STD when you have unprotected sex with someone who is already infected. "Now after reviewing the slides Rosalind, you have contracted several STDs." he said.

I was really in a daze because I still didn't fully know what he was talking about. I never heard of STDs. I just thought you could get pregnant if you didn't use a condom. Well, I do remember in high school, kids talking about getting crabs, but nothing else. It didn't seem too bad other than a lot of itching, but you take the medicine and it's all better. However, when I looked at the doctor's face, it didn't say "everything was going to be better".

"Rosalind," he said in a calm voice, "you have contracted 5 STDs." "You have Syphilis, Gonorrhea, Chlamydia, Genital Warts and Herpes."

The next five minutes of the conversation were a blur to me. The doctor was talking and showing me all kinds of pamphlets with these nasty photos. But the scary thing is that the photos looked like what I saw the day in the bathroom. It was already bad news, then the doctor said something else.

"I'm going to give you a prescription for the Syphilis, Gonorrhea and Chlamydia," he said "these diseases are very serious, however with medication they can be cured. But unfortunately, it is different with the others."

I was sitting on his every word, anticipating the rest.

"Genital Warts and Herpes are both incurable," said the doctor, "it can only be treated, not cured."

I thought I was in a dream. I kept going in and out of the conversation, praying I would wake up soon. The word incurable kept ringing in my ear like a church bell.

The doctor explained that the genital warts would have to be surgically removed by a procedure called Cryotherapy. This is when the doctor applies liquid nitrogen to the warts to freeze them. Once the warts are frozen, they can be scrapped off. Because mine were so large and plenteous, it would take a few visits to treat the warts.

The herpes didn't require any surgical procedure. There was only a prescription he could give me to ease the pain. I was experiencing an outbreak. This helped clarify the sores and white puss I saw. It was easy-to-get, but not easy to get rid of. Everything had changed!

The doctor gave me as much information as possible, before he left the room. He reminded me to schedule my next appointment as soon as possible, so we can begin the first treatment and he was gone. I stopped by the nurses' station, made an appointment, and slowly walked out.

This time the slow walk was not because of the physical pain. I was devastated. I felt nasty, embarrassed, dirty, and unclean. How could something like this happen? WHO did I get it from? Was its Hamp or Mason? Or maybe Tony. Maybe it was Johnathan. The doctor said it could be as quick as a week or as long as two months before you even notice some STDs. So that probably knocked out Hamp. This was still a nightmare. Once I finally got to my car, I sat there for the longest time holding back the tears…but it was inevitable. I cried hard and long in that parking lot. I just felt so nasty. I hated myself for being so stupid and sleeping around. I would not have pictured me dealing with this in a million years. I was too young for something like this to happen. All I wanted was to have a good time and make up for all those lost years, I couldn't take advantage off because I was a girl, but I was too young.

I had convinced myself that I was not living like this. I wanted to kill myself. I began driving around in a circle, thinking how to get in a wreck. I saw a big Oak tree and kept thinking, "if I drive the car head-on into this tree it can all be over!" I continued to drive in circles, but I could barely see beyond the tears. The cars behind me were honking like crazy, but I didn't care. I just wanted everybody to leave me alone and go to hell!

I was in such a daze just driving and crying. Suddenly, I realized I was driving on the same street Johnathan lived on. It was horrible! I was a basket case behind the wheel. Nobody cared for me, NOBODY! When I saw his house, I sped up because I didn't want to even see a glimpse of him. I needed it all to end! I just pulled over and cried for help. I couldn't go home. I didn't know what to do. I drove to the nearest pay-phone and called Yolanda.

"Hello?" it was Yolanda's dad.

"Hey Mr. Jones," I muttered, "It's Roz. Can I speak to Yolanda?"

He handed her the phone after a few seconds.

"Hey girl," she said. "what did the doctor say?"

I couldn't even talk at this point. All I could do was cry. Yolanda tried her best to calm me down, but nothing worked.

"Roz, you have to talk to me." she said, "what's the matter? Are you pregnant?"

I still couldn't form my mouth to repeat those disgusting words. I just continued to cry and ask for help.

"Ok, where are you?" Yolanda asked demandingly, "I'm coming to get you!"

I finally had a little energy to speak.

"I'm at a pay-phone Uptown," I said. "Yolanda, I can't go home."

"Come over here so we can talk." She said.

I hung up the phone and got back in the car. I was so grateful to have a friend like Yolanda. She always had my back in every situation. The simple fact that I was able to tell her what the doctor said and knowing she would not make me feel bad about myself made me feel better. I kept telling myself that once I talked to Yolanda, that she would know what to do and this day would end! As I got closer to Yolanda's house, I knew I had to get it together because her dad was home. So, it took everything inside of me to hold back the tears.

"Hey Mr. Jones," I said.

"Hey baby," he replied, "how you doing?

"I'm ok." I answered.

"So whatcha' been up to this day?" he asked, trying to start a conversation.

I really didn't want to talk to Mr. Jones. I just wanted to run to Yolanda's room and tell her what happened.

"Oh, nothing much," I said. "Mr. Jones, is Yolanda in the back?" I asked, hoping he would get the hint.

"Yeah, she back there," he said, "go on."

I quickly left before Mr. Jones started talking about work or sports or something off the wall. Now, the big problem with Yolanda's house is that there was no privacy. She lived in a 2-bedroom shotgun house. You could stand in Yolanda's living room and look straight through the entire house and see the back door, SHOTGUN! So even though I was rushing to get away from Mr. Jones, the only thing separating us was the bedroom and the bathroom. Yolanda's room didn't even have a door.

I felt like bursting into tears again, but I had to control my emotions. I could not let her parents know what was going on.

"Hey Roz," Yolanda said in a concerned voice, "what's going on?

"Yo," I whispered, "it's bad."

"Are you pregnant?" she said.

It was very hard for me to even repeat what the doctor said. I could tell Yolanda was getting worried, so I decided to let her read the pamphlets the doctor gave me. It was also better for her to read the information, because Mr. Jones wasn't that far away. Her dad already walked through the room once. Remember, it was a shotgun house so in order to get a drink of water, one had to pass through Yolanda's room to get to the kitchen.

144

I pulled out all the "fact" sheets and handed them to Yolanda.
Each time she began to read a new pamphlet, I began to cry a little harder. Finally, Yolanda read everything.

"Roz, what are you trying to tell me?" she asked.

"Yolanda," I said in a serious tone, "I have all 5 of those diseases."

The minute I told Yolanda, I began to cry as if I just found out for the first time. Just then Mr. Jones walked back to the kitchen, but this time he doesn't walk straight into the kitchen. Mr. Jones stops right by the bed.

"Rosalind," he asked, "are you ok?"

I was too embarrassed to look him directly in the eye. I just stared down at the floor and nodded my head up and down. Of course, Mr. Jones knew I wasn't alright, so he eventually left the room. This time he didn't come back. I think he finally realized Yolanda and I needed to talk. I sat there on the bed waiting for Yolanda to offer her advice. I needed her to tell me what to do. Unfortunately, and to my surprise, that never happened.

Yolanda put down all the pamphlets. She never shed a tear with me about my situation. Instead she seemed relieved. I'm not sure if Yolanda made a mistake or if she was thinking aloud, because I will NEVER forget what she said next.

"I'm glad it's not me," she said.

Yolanda knew that she wasn't always a "good girl" so for a moment, she forgot all about what I was going through. So, she really was sad for me, but extremely glad for her. My best friend, my girl, my ace boon coon, my military buddy wasn't there for me as I assumed.

It was at that moment I realized that I was about to go through this all alone.

It was a very awkward moment in the room. Yolanda wasn't talking. I was crying and hurting. Still crying about the bad report, I received from the doctor, but also hurting from Yolanda's comment.

I decided to hang around Yolanda's house for a while. Besides, I couldn't go home right away after all that crying. I looked a mess! My eyes were red and sore. No doubt if I went home too soon, my mom would suspect something was wrong. We watched television. We ate dinner. We listened to music. But we never talked about the great big elephant in the room. Somehow, we thought if we didn't talk about the challenge it would disappear. Wrong!

A few hours later, I decided to go home. As I got closer and closer to the house, I began to feel worse and worse. I was so ashamed! I felt so dirty and nasty. I felt like the minute I walk into the house my mom is going to notice something is wrong. No matter what, I knew I couldn't tell my parents. I knew they would not understand. So, I made up in my mind, I was going to hide this from my family until the day I die.

The next few days were the worse. I didn't want to do anything. I didn't want to talk to anybody. I didn't want to live anymore. 19 years old with 5 sexually transmitted diseases. What was I going to do? Who would ever want to be with me? I felt like I was tainted. Crazy thoughts kept running through mind of killing myself. I was in a constant battle. Why was I so stupid? Why did I sleep with all those guys? The most embarrassing part is that I didn't even know who I got the STDs from!

I was succeeding at hiding everything, even my thoughts of suicide from my family. I tried to be my normal self. The last thing I wanted was my mom asking me questions about why I was walking so slowly? So, whenever I came downstairs, I walked liked everything was ok. Even though I was in excruciating pain, they couldn't tell. Or better yet, why are you taking medicine? So, I hid my medicine in the closet and took it religiously. To eliminate the possibility of any questions, I stayed in my room most of the time and I swore Yolanda to secrecy and not to ever tell anybody. To this day, as far as I know, she honored my request.

The weekend was very difficult. The first outbreak is always the worst. I was in so much pain. The swelling around my thighs was inflammation of my glands, which caused a great throbbing pain. I just wanted the medicine to kick in, so I could get some relief. As for now, the only relief I could find was sleep. When I was asleep, I could escape everything.

Because of the severity of the warts, they adjusted the doctor's schedule to start my treatments Tuesday. The good part is I only had to go through 2 sessions of freezing treatments, but the worst part was that I was still dealing with the same horrible outbreak, while going through the freezing of the warts.

I had so much on my mind. I thought I was going crazy. I was on an emotional roller coaster. I was confused one second and the next minute, I was angry. Then, I was frustrated. Then I was embarrassed. I was so ashamed. I kept putting myself down. If I could have only turned back the clock, it would have been better. The biggest question I kept asking myself was this; who is going to want me? Nobody will ever want to be with me intimately. Unfortunately, all the questions I should have been concerned with like marriage, a husband, and children were now at the forefront. I knew that I was dealing with a serious issue and if I ever wanted "Mr. Right" in my life it needed to be addressed. But there was time for that. The greater issue at hand, was telling those I had been sleeping around with. I felt obligated to tell Mason. He and I were like a couple, well, somewhat. I didn't want him to think I was not interested in him anymore, so I had to tell him. But if I was going to tell Mason, I needed to tell Johnathan. Johnathan deserved to know the truth. I really cared for him. If there was any possibility, any at all, of our relationship growing, I had to be honest with him. Then there was Tony. He was the last person I slept with. It was during our night together, I began to feel bad. So, if anybody deserved to know, it should be Tony, I thought.

The next few days were very crazy. I was replaying the same story over and over and repeatedly. It was like my mind was on instant replay. Not to mention telling Mason, Johnathan, and

Tony. Why in the world did I even care about telling these guys? I could have just kept it to myself. But my conscience wouldn't let me rest. Three different phone calls, three different guys, and three different reactions.

"Hey Mason," I said softly. "It's Roz."

"What's up?" he replied. "Where were you this weekend? I didn't see you and you haven't called. Where you been?" he asked.

"Mason, I have to tell you something." I whispered.

I thought I was about to lose it. I couldn't believe I was about to tell Mason about the STDs. What in the world was he going to think?

"What's wrong?" he asked.

"Umm, Mason, I had to go to the doctor this past Friday." I explained. "It was one of those clinics for girls." I said.

"Are you pregnant?" he asked with a little excitement in his voice.

"No." I answered.

"Ok, so you why did you go to the doctor?" Mason asked.

"Look, Mason, this is really hard for me." I tried to explain.

"Something happened." "Something really bad." I said.

"Bad like what?" he asked.

Every time, I started to say something, I would get all choked up.

"I'm listening." he said.

"I know," I said, trying to get Mason to have patience.

"This is really hard." I said.

"Roz, just say it." said Mason

"I.. I…Mason, I have an STD." I muttered.

"What!" he exclaimed.

"Mason, the doctor said I have 5 STDs." I explained. "I'm so sorry."

"Are you serious?" he asked. "No, you're not serious." He said.

"Mason, I am serious." I explained. "I would never joke about this. All I know is that I started feeling bad about a month ago. I couldn't even walk without being in pain. So, I decided to see the doctor."

"Who did this to you?" he demanded. "Who did this Roz?" "I'm gonna kick their ass!"

"Mason, I don't know." I said. "It..."

I started to tell Mason, that it could have been several people. But that would have been me admitting that I was not just sleeping with him. Even though I wanted to believe I was the only person Mason was just sleeping, deep down inside I knew I wasn't. Perhaps Mason felt the same. Besides, he did ask who did this to me did, implying it was someone other than himself. I think neither one of us wanted to admit the reality of our relationship. I was a booty call in the middle of the night. He was my iron, when I needed it. There was no seriousness to our relationship. So, instead of me giving names, I just played clueless.

"It's okay." I said.

"Oh baby, I'm so sorry this happened to you." He said. "So that's why I haven't seen you. I knew something was wrong."

"Mason, you should have called if you didn't see me." I replied. "Why didn't you call?"

"Well you know baby, I been working and taking care of things around the club." He explained. 'That's all." "Look, do you want to come over? We can finish talking in person?"

"Mason, I don't want to go or do anything right now." I said. "I just need some time."

"Well, you know everything is gonna be alright?" he said. "I just wish I knew who did this to you. I'm telling you I would kick their A-S-S! I'm so pissed. You just don't deserve this!"

At this point I was crying all over again, agreeing with everything that Mason was saying. I didn't deserve this. I was a good girl. I never hurt anybody. Why was this happening to me? WHY? I was so emotional I had to get off the phone.

"Mason, look I need to go," I explained. "I'll talk to you later."

After Mason and I ended our conversation, I cried for almost an hour. I was so embarrassed. I felt so bad. The worst part was that I still had more phone calls to make. I really wanted to get this all out of the way, but I was too emotional to talk to anybody else that day. So, I decided to make a call a day. Today Mason… tomorrow Johnathan and then Tony.

I woke up early the next morning to make sure I was on time for my 9'o clock doctor's appointment. This was the first treatment for the genital warts. I was so scared because I didn't know what to expect. I was already in pain, so I couldn't imagine it getter much worse. I walked back into that doctor's office even more embarrassed. I didn't even know what to tell the nurse when I walked in the door. I just signed in and waited for my name to be called.

"Rosalind?" the nurse called. "You can come this way."

I immediately got up and followed the nurse. I walked with my head down I almost bumped into the wall. I didn't want to take any chances of anybody recognizing me. When I got into the examination room and got ready for the procedure. Before the nurse left, she tried to reassure me that everything was going to be ok. Waiting for the doctor to arrive felt like eternity. I was nervous. Suddenly, I heard movement on the other side of the door.

"Good Morning Rosalind", the doctor said as he walked in. "How are you today?'

I thought to myself, "I'm about to have warts frozen and scrapped of my body…. it's not a good day."

"I'm okay but kinda scared." I replied with my tears in my eyes.

"The procedure won't take too long," the doctor explained. "I just need you to lay back and try to relax." "I promise I will talk you through everything."

I'm not sure if this made me feel better or worse. It was all too embarrassing. I should not be here. No 19-year-old should be in the doctor's office preparing to have warts frozen scrapped from her body. No 19-year-old should be thinking about suicide. No 19-year-old should be scared to talk to her parents out of fear of being rejected, fussed at, or misunderstood. No 19-year-old should be receiving this death sentence!!

The procedure didn't take hours. In fact, it was over in about 30 minutes and I survived. One treatment finished and still two more treatments to go. I got dressed and headed toward the nurse's station to schedule my next appointment. I wanted to stay on track no matter how embarrassed I was.

As I was leaving the clinic, I began thinking to myself, should I call Johnathan or Tony? I didn't want them walking in the dark about what happened to me and that they could now be in potential risk. As hard it was for me, I knew I needed to make the call. RING, RING, RING...

Rebound Pt. 2

At this point it seemed to be the lowest stage in my life. I just wanted to forget! If there was any way to go back with an eraser and change all the mistakes, I would have done it in a heartbeat. Doctor's appointments! Prescriptions! Outbreaks! Pain! Stress! Agony! Embarrassment! Shame! Disgust! Stupidity! Lies! Secrecy! These are the words that I would be associated with forever.

Yolanda and I continued to go out every now and then, but it wasn't the same. I had finally pulled away from Mason, Johnathan and Tony and accepted the fact that all my hopes and dreams of a committed relationship were shattered. No matter where I went, I always felt ashamed and embarrassed. I was still taking medication for herpes outbreaks. If I had an outbreak, I would just get a prescription and it clears up in a few days and back to the same routine. Most times I felt nasty. I was smiling and laughing on the outside, but I was crying uncontrollably on the inside. If I wasn't crying on the inside, I was screaming for help.

One night we decided to hang out in the Quarters, drinking and hanging out, no real agenda whatsoever and that's when I met him. He wasn't drop dead gorgeous, but he was very confident and that attracted me! He was standing by the street pole as we were passing by and he invited himself into our conversation. What I thought was going to be a simple interaction, lasted for about 30 minutes.

He and I talked as if we had been knowing each other for a while. Maybe things were about to finally change. It was like he and I were the only two people outside. We were into each other…major chemistry! I could tell Yolanda was getting a little frustrated, but I just couldn't stop laughing at his jokes. Every time we tried to end the conversation another topic came up! This was the best interaction I had with a guy in weeks outside of my airing out my dirty laundry. I was not about to let him pass me by. I didn't throw myself at him, but I laughed at all his jokes, made eye contact and made sure the attention was on me. Finally, we realized this could be leading to something. His name was Michael, but his friends called him Mike.

"So, this conversation could go on all night," Mike said. "why don't you give me your number and we can finish it later?"

I immediately gave him my number and anticipated a call. The rest of the night no matter where Yolanda and I went, I couldn't stop thinking

about Mike. His was so full of life. He was

talkative and funny. I wanted to end our night of bar hopping EARLY

so I could get home and wait for Mike's phone call. Yolanda dropped

me off around 1am. I got dressed for bed and dozed off. Around 2:30am.. Ring, Ring, Ring…

"Hello?" I answered in a questionable voice, but deep down I

already knew it was Mike. I was excited to hear his voice.

"Yeah, Rosalind?" he asked.

"It's me", I said relieved that he really called. "I'm glad you called."

"I told you I would." He replied.

"You do know it's almost 3am?" I said in an enticing voice.

His response was, "I'm just getting started at this time."

We stayed in deep conversation until after 6am talking about…. well mainly him.

Mike could talk.

Outside of the basics…where do you live, what's your favorite color, food, car etc. He talked about him.

His desire was to be a male model. I could picture that happening for Mike. He was decent looking, he had great charisma, swag and a ton of confidence. He struck me as being the life of the party.

Later, my assumption proved to be right. What started off as a, let's get to know each other call tonight and see where this leads us…. started happening night after night after night and eventually day after day.

I saw potential in Mike. He seemed like someone I wanted as a boyfriend.

He worked. He had his own apartment. He loved to drink and party!! My kind of guy. Mike introduced me to New Orleans in a fun way. Mike was fun to be around. He worked in the French Quarter as a waiter at a world-renowned restaurant. He interacted with all classes of people, but mainly the wealthy. This is where he desired to be.

Whenever we would go out, it had to be the best, the top of the line. He was a first-class type of guy. Some people would call it living above your means, but Mike felt like this…. If I'm good enough to serve the food, then I'm good enough to sit and enjoy the food. He believed he should have the best. He never wanted to be treated like he was less than, so I tried my best to support him in any way I possibly could.

I learned during our very first phone conversation, which lasted 'til 6 o'clock in the morning, that he had a horrible experience growing up. When he was a toddler, he witnessed a loved one's life tragically taken away. Imagine that the one who was supposed to always be there and care for you was instantly gone. But what was worse is that they died at the hands of another loved one. With his mom forever gone and dad now in jail, he was a product of the foster care system. His foster parents were much, much older than his biological parents. But they treated him so special. Ms. Virginia was his original foster mother who eventually adopted Mike. She was close friends with his biological parents and would always help them out financially when they hit "hard times." Unfortunately, his dad had a bad drinking problem and let the situation take control of him. It was during one of the times when the alcohol was winning that his dad took the life of his mother. So, the relationship that was formed between his parents and Ms. Virginia was transferred to Mike. She was a jewel and we "connected" instantly.

Mike and I would talk on the phone every morning and every night. If we weren't on the phone with each other, I would be hanging out at his house. It also became my escape to be an adult. There were just too many rules at my parents' house. It was totally different when I was with Mike. He had been on his own for quite some time. Mike and I started spending all our time together. I had practically moved in with him after a few short weeks of dating. I felt so grown. Instead of going home after class, I would go to his apartment to study and relax. Most times he had to be at work for 3o'clock, so I would drop him off at work and go back to the apartment. I would cook, clean, and prep the bedroom with all sorts of surprises and gadgets. Then at midnight head out to pick him up. Once he got off at midnight, of course we didn't go immediately back to the house. We would hang out with his co-workers drinking and laughing 'til 2 or 3 in the morning. My mom would always want me to come home by a certain time and I hated that. So, in the beginning of me "dating" Mike, I would call her, around midnight, and say that I'm staying out late. Hoping she didn't ask where I was or who I was going to be with.

Ring, Ring, Ring

"Ummm, hello," in her who the hell is this calling my house at midnight voice.

"Yeah Ma, it's me. You don't need to wait up because I'll be out a little later." I said.

"Rosalind, you know I'm going to lock the door by 2am. Where are you?" she said.

"I'm just hanging out with Mike and his friends, Yolanda is here also, so I'll probably sleep by her house. I'll be home tomorrow after my last class." I replied.

"Alright Roz." Momma said.

After we ended our call, I would immediately call Yolanda, so she could cover for me, just in case ANYTHING happened! Yolanda and I were inseparable until Mike came into the picture. For whatever reason, she didn't particularly like him. So, I would call and beg her to "vouch" for me. She would, but reluctantly.

This pattern continued for a while until it was quite evident to everybody that I was sleeping over at Mike's house. The late-night partying increased and the phone calls to my mom saying I would be out late or sleeping by Yolanda slowly decreased. I was having fun and really didn't feel like I needed to "check-in" with anyone. Eventually, the only time I came home was to pick up more and more of my clothes.

Things were going great between Mike and me. He began saying how much he cared for me and how I was "good" for him. I was hearing wedding bells and picking out a gown in my mind but, there were two HUGE obstacles…my parents and my past. First the parents…. Well, it had been at least two or three months since Mike and I started dating, if that's what you call it. I really thought it was time for him to meet my parents. This was the first person I wanted my family to meet. I knew this was the one!! There was one problem. They didn't like him at all. Since Mike had his own place, I spent a lot of time away from home and by his apartment. I would leave on a Friday night and would not come back home for 2 days. Eventually the two days turned into 4 days. Four days then turned into a week. I was practically living with Mike.

We got up every day like a married couple. I would go to class and he would hang around doing chores at the house until it was time for him to go to work. He was a food server in a famous family owned restaurant. His work day didn't start until 3pm and ended most nights at 2am. I loved it because I would drop him off at work then hang out at his house all night…PEACE AND QUIET!! I would study and then change into a cute sexy outfit and pick him up from work, so we could hang out drinking and partying with his co-workers. So yeah, mom guess who's coming to dinner???!!!

I called my mom and told her Mike and I were coming over.

"Hey Ma, whatcha doing?" I asked very reserved.

"I'm watching tv, why?" she answered. "Where are you?"

"I'm about to come over to the house for a little while," I replied.

"Uh huh," she said.

"But I'm not by myself, ok?" I hinted. "Mike is coming with me. I really want you to meet him momma."

"Roz, I don't want to meet no boy that doesn't respect your parents!" Momma said in a stern voice.

"Ma, it's not like that," I tried to explain. "He does respect you. I made the decision to stay away. So, can you please let him come over?" I begged.

"Roz y'all can come over, but he can't stay for long." Momma said.

I didn't tell Mike about the conversation my mom and I had. I wanted him to be comfortable and welcome. After all, this was it. I knew once we all sat down to talk, everything was going to change. Mike was off this night, so we decided we would go over by my parents before hanging out with our friends. I was so excited they would finally get a chance to meet him. All the way over, I'm prepping Mike on what to say and what not to say. I'm telling him how to get my parents to like him. Praying for a miracle because the earlier conversation between my mom and I set the tone for a mess.

"Hey daddy!" I said as I walked in the house.

Mike was following closely behind me.

"Daddy this is Mike," I cheerfully said. "Mike this is my daddy," in a school girl voice.

Mike extended his hand as any gentleman would and introduced himself.

"How ya doing Mr. Armstrong," Mike said. "It's good to finally meet you."

"Yeah good to meet you too." My daddy said.

I knew not much conversation was about to take place between Mike and my dad, so I grabbed Mike by the hand and led him into the other room where my mom was.

"Momma, this is Mike," I said. "Mike, this is my mom, Mrs. Armstrong."

Mike, once again, extended his hand and greeted my mom.

"Hi Mrs. Armstrong, how are you?" Mike asked. "You have a nice home," trying to make conversation.

"I'm fine Mike," said my mom. "You and Rosalind have been spending a lot of time together. What's your plan for my daughter?" my mom asked

I could not believe she asked that. I already knew that she wasn't fond of Mike because we had been practically living together. Also, my mom was strictly by the book...the Good Book!! My grandfather was a Baptist preacher, a reverend as a matter of fact. All my mom's male siblings were deacons in the church. Mom took us to church every Sunday. We went to youth choir rehearsal every Saturday. Not to mention, every summer, we attended vacation bible school. So, she had a lot of questions for Mike.

"Well Mrs. Armstrong," Mike said after clearing his throat. "I like your daughter a lot. We just kickin' it for now, you know." My mom didn't seem to be satisfied with that answer. It wasn't anything she said, but looks are truly worth 1000 words! I knew I had to break up the tension.

"Ma, whatcha cooked?" I asked with anticipation. "Mike, you want something to eat? My mom is a great cook." "Yeah, I'm a little hungry." Mike replied.

"There's some left-over in the frig Roz," mom answered. "You can fix something for y'all."

I got up quickly and went into the kitchen. I wanted Mike to come with me, but at the same time I didn't want it to be obvious that I didn't want momma to interrogate him anymore. So, I left him in the den with momma. It was very quiet. I had to hurry. Once I prepared the plates, I quickly re-joined Mike and momma in the den.

As Mike and I ate, we did more talking to each other, than him talking to my mom. My dad stayed in the living room. I already knew he had little or nothing to say to Mike. I never tried to force that issue. After about an hour, I knew it was time to make our departure.

"Well Momma, Mike and I are gonna get ready to go," I said. "We are meeting some friends and we don't want to be late."

"Thank you for the food Mrs. Armstrong. It was good." Mike said.

"Thanks, and you're welcome." Momma said.

I could tell my mom wanted to say more, a lot more, but she decided not to bother. She knew that I really liked Mike and that I had my mind made up that he was the one.

"Ok Ma, we're going," I said. "I'll call you later, ok?"

"Alright, Roz," Momma said. "Be careful."

"It was nice meeting you Mrs. Armstrong," Mike said. "Mr. Armstrong," Mike said as he extended his hand. "Y'all take care."

"Yeah, Mike same here," my dad answered for both he and the Mrs.

I knew my parents didn't care for Mike. But the meeting needed to take place because he was going to be around for quite some time. Like I said earlier, I was falling for Mike. There was serious chemistry between us, but I was very reserved of moving forward because of my parents and my past. I finally, had the "meet my parents" but he still didn't know the full extent of my past. I was still taking medication for the herpes. It was an ongoing battle. Any type of stress would cause my body to react negatively. I had to tell him this weekend.

It was Friday night and Mike was finally off from the restaurant. On his off nights, he loved to hang out with his other co-workers that were off. We would party and walk through the Quarters, drink fine wine, and let the good times roll. Mike's main concern is that I looked sexy ALL THE TIME. He liked when his co-workers complimented me on how well I looked. At times, it was like I was a prize to Mike. So, the hair, clothes, nails, toes etc. had to be 100%!! The sexier, the better. The tighter, the better. I was his trophy. But this night was different. Things were moving fast, and I wanted to slow down for a minute and talk to him about my past. Here goes….

"Mike, where are we going tonight?" I asked like a kid on Christmas waiting to hear what Santa got for them.

"There's this new bar down in the quarters I've been wanting us to go to." He said. "We can swing by the restaurant and get some appetizers with my discount and then head over to the bar to shoot some pool. You ok with that?" He asked.

"Sounds good to me!" I said cheerfully. "Mike, I do want to talk to you about something before we leave," now changing the tone in voice.

"Ok, but first let me see what you are wearing." He said. "Man, you look good! I can't wait to show you off tonight!" he said. "But wait, let's get a drink." He said while headed towards the kitchen. Mike was a big lush. He always kept beer, wine, and Jack Daniels in the cabinet.

He came back with two glasses of red wine and sat so we could really begin our conversation.

"Mike, look." I said hesitantly. "ummm…. you know I'm not really that nice little uptown girl you think I am."

"Girl, what are you talking about?" he said with this puzzled look on his face. "I told Jaz we would be at the bar around 12:30." He said.

"I'm trying to say it." I said reluctantly. "This is really difficult to say Mike."

"I don't know what you're talking about. Difficult to say what?" he said confusingly.

I was struggling to get the words out of my mouth, but I could tell Mike was confused and starting to get impatient. So, I took a deep breath and finally said it.

"Mike, I kinda slept around A LOT before I met you…and…well…ummm…ummm." I tried to say.

'Roz, what are you talking about?" he said.

"I kinda, when I was you know sleeping with this one and that one, kinda contracted an STD." I said.

"Ok, so you're alright, right?" He asked.

"Well, yes and no." I answered "I had several and I still have challenges from time to time. That's why I asked you to use a condom. I don't want to put you at any risk." I explained.

He seemed to be ok with my news. Not a lot of questions. No big reaction. He finished his glass of wine and said, "Ok, you're ready?"

"Yeah, sure, I guess." I said.

His reaction was very unexpected. He was so concerned about meeting up with Jaz and the others that he barely commented on what I just said. I didn't know what to think.

We went out that night and as usual met up with his friends. We were having a great time shooting pool and drinking. Everything seemed fine. My earlier news didn't even seem to faze Mike.

Once we partied 'til we couldn't go anymore, he and I went back to his apartment and had an even better time.

This routine of working hard during the week and living for the weekend continued for quite some time. He was the life of the party. It was never a dull moment when he was around. He always had energy and drive. He reminded me of Clark Kent. He was a hard worker during the day and transformed into another person at night. I would see the fatigue on his face, but he never let that stop him from having fun. Before we would leave the house, Mike would take a long hot bath then primp in the mirror. Sometimes he would be in the bathroom for 2 hours getting ready. It was a metamorphosis. Things finally seemed like they started coming together for us. Even though I was still having physical challenges, Mike really didn't care. I just chose not to talk about it. If I needed medicine, I took it and got back to enjoying life.

We were getting along well, but every now and then Mike would get really frustrated at little things. He had a temper and absolutely no patience. He would snap at me if I forgot to do something, but in the next 30 minutes he would be back to normal. He would step away and go to the bathroom, to calm down, then back to himself. Sometimes, even more cheerful.

One night as we were out hanging with his friends, his behavior was a little different. Normally Mike would keep his eyes on me the entire night. I was his "show piece," his "trophy." He would constantly brag about me in front of me to his boys. But this night was different. Not just this night, but many nights it became strange.

We would be sitting, talking, drinking and having fun then, suddenly, Mike would leave for 15 minutes or longer while I was left at the table with his friends. He would go to the restroom, most times by himself. But if it wasn't to the restroom and by himself, he would go with a friend. If not to the restroom, with a friend, then outside to sit in somebody's car. It started to happen every time we would go out. I'm just left sitting there. When Mike finally did come back, he would be mellow for a few minutes, then hype man. It was really weird because he would be "the life of the party" then come back partying for life.

This pattern not only happened when we were hanging out, but it started to occur at the apartment. We always ended the night with a glass of wine or a beer. Mike and I would be sitting on the couch talking about our day and he would get up and go to the bathroom. He would be in the bathroom for a very, very long time. It was almost the same scenario. He come back into the living room, a little laid back, but after a few minutes he would get a second burst of energy. He would just start talking and talking and talking…OMG!! It would be 3am and he was still talking. Unfortunately, we also started to argue and bicker about silly things. But after one or two drinks, and Mike's field trip to the bathroom, he got aggravated quicker.

Red flags were going up. Mike seemed to be involved in something and whatever that something was, it was in the bathroom.

One night while we were out, I started noticed how his behavior changed when certain friends came around. He was no longer with me, but it was like he was on a date with them. It was as if he had some type of allegiance to them. He would offer to buy them drinks. He as always complementing them. It was a site to see. Then of course, they would disappear and go to the restroom or outside together. His friend Jackie was a sweet guy. He was married with two small children, but I didn't have a good feeling about him at all.

Mike was clearly in some sort of cahoots with Jackie. It was an awkward relationship between the two. My instincts were telling me that Mike was using some type of drug. Marijuana to be exact. I used to "puff, puff, pass" myself so the calm, mellow mood was familiar. I just kept monitoring his behavior at the apartment and when we were around his friends.

His mood swings were becoming more and more frequent that it was almost irritating to be at his house. But because I loved him so much, I continued to try and work through things. I was helping to pay rent and buy groceries. Whatever was necessary to keep the peace and show Mike how much I was willing to be with him. Unfortunately, it didn't stop his behavior. So, I had to take it a step further. One day I made up my mind that I was going to find out what he was up to. I finished class early and came straight to the apartment. I had a plan.

"Hey" I said as I entered the apartment.

Mike was just chilling watching something on tv and getting ready for work.

"You home early?" he said. "I thought you had to work tonight." He asked.

"No, the event was canceled, so I can rest tonight and catch up on some reading." I explained.

"Ok. I'll be ready soon." He said.

Mike even had his personal chauffeur, ME! He never learned how to drive so he was very excited that I not only knew how to drive but had a car. Well, a piece of a car and I loved my two-toned Bertha. It was a Monte Carlo with a blue hood and a brown everything else. Like I said earlier, it was truly a destination car. It got me from Point A to Point B!! Anyway, Mike didn't have to worry about anything. I was covering all the loose ends in his life.

"Roz, you ready?" Mike asked.

"Yeah we can leave now to beat the downtown traffic." I said.

The conversation in the car was very light this day. He seemed to snap at the littlest things, so I decided to start and wait for him to bring up the topics of conversation.

"Dr. Maury came by the apartment today to do an inspection. He noticed some of your things around the house." He said.

"Was that a problem? Dr. Maury notices everything." I said.

No, he didn't say anything, but he hinted that my girlfriend's car is always outside the house. He asked if you were living there." He explained.

"Well, I'm sure you told him no." I said.

"I'm not stupid Rosalind, damn!" he shouted. "You always start with me and I'm not for it today!" he said.

"Mike, I know you wouldn't say that. What's wrong with you?" I asked. "You are so touchy and tense." I shouted.

"Listen, I got a lot on my mind...the rent is due. Dr. Maury is lurking around. Hours are short. I'm just frustrated Roz and I don't need you asking stupid ass questions or making stupid ass remarks!" he said.

"Everything will be alright. I'll help with the rent and Dr. Maury will not find out that I'm there...it's between You and I, ok?" I said to assure him.

"Alright Roz." He said.

The rest of the ride was quiet. I said to myself, this man is crazy. What in the world was going on inside of his mind? I knew once I got back to that apartment, it was on! I dropped Mike off and bee-lined it back home. CIA don't have anything on a woman with a plan.

I went inside and started looking in the bedroom, in his closet, and in the dresser drawers for anything I could find. Nothing! I looked in the kitchen cabinets and nothing but alcohol and the groceries I purchased. Other than that, Nothing! I looked in the bathroom, which seemed to be the hang out spot and at first everything was in order. Until I opened the small medicine cabinet. The cabinet was so thin and narrow, we didn't keep much in there. But it was enough space....

There were razor blades and a white powder looking substance on the bottom shelf of this tiny medicine cabinet. I was alarmed! The white powder was divided into thin lines, almost strips. I was so scared I froze for a minute. I wasn't expecting to see that. As I was standing there in the bathroom, I had a flashback of the past few weeks in my mind. All the trips to the bathroom... the times at home and when we were out. The constant sniffling! It was as if Mike always had the sniffles at night. The mood swings...it was all starting to make sense. The disappearances, it was starting to make sense. It was the "WHY are you experimenting with this stuff" that didn't make any sense. Maybe I'm over reacting. Maybe this isn't what I think it is...how can I tell? I didn't want to approach Mike. He was so tense these days, it would only make matters worse. I was confused. Hurt! Angry! What had I gotten myself into?

I just sat for the rest of the night contemplating IF I was going to address the issue with Mike. But what was I going to say? "Hey Bae, how was your night and by the way, how long have you been snorting?" Or, "hey bae, how was work? Did you meet anybody new? Did you buy any drugs? How much is the light bill that you need me to pay because I know you spent all your money sniffing it up!!" Help Me Somebody! What the Hell?! The time was getting near that I should be on my way to pick up Mike from work. I took a very slow drive because I was trying to avoid seeing him any sooner than I had to. I felt so stupid.

"Hey Bae, how was work?" I asked as Mike got into the car.

"It was fine." he said. "Let's stop and get a beer from Lucy's." he suggested.

"Ok, but only for a little while" I responded.

I was still messed up in my mind about what I found earlier. Still praying that it wasn't true. We hung out for a short while, shooting pool, and drinking. At least Mike was drinking, I didn't want anything, other than the truth. But I was too scared to bring it up. So, I ignored it.

Days and weeks went by and Mike continued his "habit." I really wasn't trying to wonder anymore. The facts were clear. Most days, it seemed to be under control. At least I thought it was under control. Mike began needing me to pitch in with the bills a little more now than a few weeks ago. He kept saying he wasn't making much in tips. This pissed me off because I knew where the extra money was being spent. I did what I could do to help, but he was not trying to make up the lost wages any kind of way. Unfortunately, the arguments and snapping at one another continued. I just kept telling myself it was going to change. Then I kept asking myself when will it change? Is he taking advantage of me? Does he really love me and want to be with me? It's more than the sex and money, Roz. Right? I decided to test it.

173

I decided to stop with the thrills and frills at night and go to sleep. If a bill was left on the table that said past due, I pretended to not even notice it. Eventually it got paid without me offering any assistance. As difficult as it was, and as much as I didn't want to do it, I decided to go home and stay there for a few days. We needed space. I needed a break.

"Roz?" it was Mike on the other end of the phone.

"Hey Mike, what's up?" I said.

"What's up? Roz what's going on? I'm here by myself and you didn't bother to call!" Mike asked.

"I told you I was going to stay by my parents the other night when I dropped you off at work, remember?" I explained.

"Yeah, but it's been two days. What's wrong?" He asked.

This was my opportunity to tell Mike how I've been feeling and ask him what was going on with him. But I didn't.

"Mike, I just decided to catch up on some things at home." I explained. "You know I have exams coming up soon."

"Ok, but you could have studied here like you always do, Roz" he said. "Look, I'm not crazy and I know something is wrong. You've been acting weird lately." Mike explained.

"I'll be back tomorrow night and we can…" I was saying before Mike interrupted.

"Are you seeing somebody else?" Mike sternly said.

"What?!" I asked in shocked.

"I know you in college and you got all those Alpha Dogs and Kappa Gamma men running behind you. I know that's what you want!" Mike yelled.

"Mike, I'm not seeing anybody else. You're tripping" I replied.

"Just because I came home doesn't mean I'm seeing somebody else.

"Then when are you coming back?" he asked.

"I was trying to tell you tomorrow before you cut me off!", I said.

"Look Roz, I was thinking when you get back, we should just go out have a good time." he suggested.

Mike knew I was getting frustrated, so he decided we needed to go out, just he and I to talk and enjoy each other, like we used to do when we first hooked up.

"We can go to Broadway and use my employee discount. I want you to get the best treatment." He said.

"Ok, that sounds good." I said with a little excitement.

The next morning, I got my things together and left for campus. As soon as I finished my last class, I called Mike.

"Hey Honey, I'm on my way to the house." I said.

"Ok. I miss you yeah, Roz." He said.

On the drive to the apartment, I was getting a little excited about seeing Mike. Even though he had been aggravating these past few weeks, the chemistry never left. By this time, I couldn't wait to see Mike.

When I got to the apartment, there was little to be said because we were all over each other like two teenagers on prom night. We had an enjoyable time as always. Perhaps things will be different since I was gone for a few days. I just wanted Mike to not take me for granted and prayerfully come clean with his behavior and private dealings, so we could move forward.

When we got to the restaurant, everyone was pleasant and excited to see Mike. As I said, he was always the life of the party and they loved him at work. Mike made everyone acknowledge him and he let it be known he was in the house. The servers took real good care of us. The food was good. Mike and I were working on us. "Roz look I know I've been tensed lately but it has nothing to do with you. I'm just trying my best to stay on top of it at work, so I can pay the bills. You know I'm also trying to get my modeling career off the ground. It's moving slow." He said. "But most importantly, you. I don't like what's been going on between us. You're important to me."

"Mike, you're important to me as well. You know that." I said.

"So, you're not going to leave me?" He asked.

"No, I'm not leaving." I said. "I just want us to be open, honest, and respectful towards each other." I explained.

"Of course, Roz." Mike answered. "So, you got my back and I have yours, right?" he asked.

"Yes Mike, you are correct." I replied agreeing with his statement. Once we decided we both wanted to work towards a better relationship, the awkwardness and tension decreased. We continued eating and laughing. Hours had past.

"You ready?" Mike asked.

"Yes, it been a long day." I said.

Mike nodded to the server, so he could bring the final check to the table. He looked over everything and made sure his employee discount was there. Things were going good until the check came to the table.

Mike began feeling around in his pocket and patting himself like he was on fire or something. All the while, I'm thinking to myself, you have got to be kidding me. I know this is not happening. I waited so Mike could address the issue.

"Roz," he said in worried tone. "I don't have my wallet." He said.

"Are you sure?" I said. "Maybe you left it in the car?" I suggested.

"No, I think I left it." He said.

"What are you going to do?" I asked.

I was very upset at this point because Mike has tried this before and I always paid for the dinner. Not this time. I refused. It wasn't my idea to come to dinner. I guess he'll be washing dishes because I'm not doing it anymore.

"Roz, can you cover it until I get paid next week?" He asked.

"Where is your wallet?" I asked. "I don't have enough to cover it sorry." I said.

"Girl stop playing." He said. "What do you mean? You always carry extra money." He explained.

I just sat there looking at Mike like he had lost his mind. Here we are again back to square one. It seemed like things were changing for the better but now this. This was ridiculous! It was a test and I must past this test. Ok, girlfriend, but in my Star Wars voice, "may the force be with you because I ain't paying for shit!"

It was crazy because for the next 2 minutes he and I just sat there staring at one another. It was almost like an ole' western scene to see who was going to pull out their pistol first, only somebody had to cough up some money. After a few minutes of me holding on to my purse for dear life, the server came back to the table and a miracle happened.

"Yo man, can I take that?" he said gesturing to remove the bill fold with the payment.

Without saying a word, Mike reached into his jacket pocket and pulled out his wallet that was full of cash!! The miracle was that he and I didn't start arguing and cause a bad scene in the restaurant like Ike and Tina Turner at the diner. I just looked at Mike holding back the tears. I was speechless as I watched Mike put the cash in the bill fold and the server whisked it away.

"Girl, what's wrong with you?" Mike asked. "Why you have that look on your face?" he said.

I guess I was in total shock because in my mind I was saying a LOT, but nothing was coming out. Perhaps that was a good thing!!

"Roz, I know you didn't believe me and think I wanted you to pay for dinner?" he asked. "Girl you are tripping." he chuckled. Ha Ha HELL!! I'm not laughing. If there was a joke, then I missed it because I was not laughing at the situation. Mike clearly wanted me to cover the cost but now it was a joke. At this point, I just wanted to leave and somehow move forward. The problem is that

I LOVED this man. Most times he could do NO WRONG in my sight.

"You want to go get a drink or shoot some pool after we leave?" Mike asked.

"Not really, let's just go back to the house. Maybe we can watch a movie or something?" I said.

The server returned, and he and Mike joked around a while. Then Mike had to make his grand exit. He went around the entire restaurant and even in the kitchen to let everyone know that he was leaving. I was in a daze somewhat. I still couldn't believe what happened earlier. I just wanted to get back to the house and move on. While he was off prepared to leave, I decided to wait by the hostess stand in the front

"Cindy, where did Mike go?" I asked.

"I'm not sure. Knowing Mike, he's probably in the bathroom telling those people he's leaving." she said jokingly.

I sat and waited for a little while longer, then I heard Mike's voice. I looked up and noticed he had that same look on his face after he would be in the bathroom for a long time. Same ole craziness.

"Mike you ready?" I asked.

"Yeah, let's go." He said in a very calm voice.

"You want to stop and rent a movie on the way home?" I asked,

"I guess that's fine, but who's gonna pay for it since you claim you don't have any money?" he asked in a sarcastic tone.

"Mike, the cost of a movie rental is a whole lot cheaper than a three-course dinner, plus wine." I said. Why are you bringing that up? Remember, you were just joking about me paying." I said.

"Yeah, Yeah, Yeah, I see you still tripping," Mike said.

"I'm not tripping! You suggested we go to dinner! You picked the place! You ordered everything on the menu and the fancy bottle of wine! You, not ME!" I yelled.

"What the hell is wrong with you?" he shouted. "I said I was joking but once again yo' ass bring shit to another level! DAMN!" he shouted. "Can we just go get the damn movie please and move on?" he suggested.

I just decided to be quiet because I knew we were about to start a serious argument. Mike was buzzed and probably high. I knew it was best I remained quiet. We went to Blockbuster. What is Blockbuster, you ask?? A long time ago, this was a movie rental store. Everyone went to blockbuster to "rent" a movie. You would go home and watch it in the comfort of your home for less than $5 a day. Again, a long time ago…RIP Blockbuster. We tried to move on but there was still tension in the air. After we finally made a few selections, we headed to the register.

I was so upset that I really didn't want to even pay a few dollars for the movie rental because of Mike's behavior. He clearly lied and wanted to pretend and push it under the rug. Maybe we will be able to address it in a few days when all the alcohol wears off.

So, we finally made it back to the house after little to no conversation on the ride home. The minute we get inside Mike said he was going to the bathroom.

"Roz, I'm going to bathroom. All that wine got me going." He said.

"Ok." I said. "I'll get the movies ready. Don't be long Mike." I said.

Mike was, as usual, in the bathroom for a long time. I just told myself whatever is going on with Mike, I'll help him get through this. When he came out of the bathroom there was a glare in his eyes. He went straight in the kitchen to pour a glass of wine.

"Bae, you want something to drink?" he asked.

I was hesitant at first because I wanted to just deal with this issue. I decided I was going to talk to him tonight. We can't keep pretending that he doesn't have a problem.

"Yes, I sure do." I replied.

Meanwhile, I was trying to get the DVD to work. It was temperamental. At times you had to play around with it to get it to work. It kept going in and out. Mike came into the room and handed me a glass of wine.

"Thank you," I said.

"Is it working?" Mike asked.

"Yup, I think it's good." I said.

We climbed into the bed to get comfortable and watch the movie. At some point, I was going to have that talk. The movie started playing but after 10 minutes it stopped again.

"Aww man." I said. "Let me try to see what is wrong." I explained.

"Roz, I thought you said you fixed it?" Mike asked.

"Well apparently, I thought it was fixed Mike." I replied sarcastically.

I had no idea what I was doing. I was just unplugging and plugging in the cord. Turning the TV off and on. I was NOT good at fixing anything electronic, but Mike was simply pathetic at anything that involved working with his hands. He always thought he was too pretty for manual labor, so I looked like a GENIUS!

"So, what's the problem?" Mike asked as he went back to the kitchen to refill his wine.

"I have no idea Mike." I said. "It's not coming back on." I turned it off and on, but that's not working." I explained.

"I guess not!" he yelled. "What the hell you think unplugging and plugging in the DVD will do?" he screamed.

I didn't even bother to turn around and deal with the foolishness. I just decided to re-connect a few wires and hope that does the trick. All the while Mike was in the kitchen fussing and complaining. Finally, I had to say something.

"Instead of you griping and complaining, maybe if you come and take a look, perhaps we can figure it out together." I said.

"No, you do it because you're the smart one, remember?! You're the one in college around all the smart people, remember! You're the one that could have gotten a new DVD because you know the thing doesn't work right all the time. Oh, but I forgot, you don't have any money." Mike yelled.

"Mike would you please for Pete's sake, let it go!" I said.

It finally started working. Mike came back into the bedroom and I knew he was high. So, we both just sat down and began watching the movie.

"POP!" the DVD went out again.

I got up to look at the DVD player again and Mike was muttering things under his breath. I just ignored it. I kneeled to look at the back connections.

"I think its broke Mike." I said.

"So, you can't fix it?" he asked sarcastically.

"No." I said while getting up.

"Stupid ass!" Mike said.

"What!" I said.

Immediately while I was getting up, Mike walked up behind me and punched me in the back of my head.

"Stupid ass!" Mike yelled.

I was so disoriented. My head was spinning. I just started screaming like a crazy person. I was angry! He didn't have to put his hands on me!

"MIKE!" I yelled. "What the fuck is wrong with you! You are a dead man!" I yelled.

"I told you don't ever put your hands on me!" I said. "I going to call my dad and he is going to kick yo ass!" I yelled!

"Roz, look I'm sorry! Let's talk!", he yelled!

Mike tried to grab my arm, so I wouldn't leave.

"Get you mother f…… hands off me Mike!" I screamed. "I hate you!" I yelled.

I was enraged! I was hurt! I was confused! I had so many emotions running through my body!

One thing I knew about a man and a woman and that was, a man, a REAL man, never puts his hands on a woman. If he did, then he wasn't a man!

I'll never forget one morning, years ago when I was a little girl around the age of 9 or 10, I think, I remember being in the car with my mom and we were going to church. Back in those days, we didn't have cell phones, iPad, or headphones to entertain us. It was either go to sleep or look out the window at street signs. I was doing just that, looking at houses, cars and street signs, when we passed this little white house with a chain fenced around it. Suddenly, just as we were passing by, there was a lady that ran out of her front door in a house coat and slippers trying to get out of the gate, when a man, I guess her husband, ran out after her and grabbed her by her bush and started hitting her. She was screaming for somebody to help her. She was trying to get away. That was over 35 years ago, and that memory is still in my mind like it was yesterday. I remember being so confused but having a sadness in my heart for that lady. My mom's response left me speechless.

"Momma, why is that man hitting that lady?" I asked while turning my head so fast to keep an eye on her while we drove past. "Cat, that's between a husband and a wife." She said while we drove past.

I didn't fully understand what she meant. I wanted to help that lady. I was scared, but I wanted to help her. To this very day whenever I'm on that street, I remember the house and re-play that eerie scene in my mind. I often wonder what happened to that lady. Did she get away? Did he hurt her? Did anybody stop to help her? Why didn't we stop?

People back in those days were so private. You never let anybody know what was going on in your house. I always remember my momma saying, what goes on behind closed doors stays behind closed doors. In other words, you better not tell anybody what was going on in your house. Apparently, that meant even when somebody's life was in danger. That's the only explanation I could think of after I called my dad to tell him Mike hit me.

I left the house yelling and screaming! I told Mike he was a dead man for putting his hands on me!

I rushed out and drove a few blocks away from the house to use the pay phone at the gas station.

RING RING RING

"Hello," my dad said as he answered the phone.

"Hey daddy," I said in my trembling voice.

"Cat, what's the matter?" he asked.

"Daddy, Mike hit me." I said and burst into tears.

"He hit you?" my dad said surprisingly.

"Yeah," I said.

"Well what happened Cat? Where are you?" he asked.

"We got into a disagreement and he hit me." I explained.

185

It was crazy because my dad wasn't responding like I thought he would. He never said he was on his way. He never got upset. He never asked if I was ok. I didn't understand.

"Daddy, can you come?" I hesitantly asked.

"No, Cat, look you just need to come home, ok." he said.

"I'ma come home but later. I need to go back and get my things." I said. "I'll call you later." I said.

"Alright Cat," he said and hung up the phone.

I sat in my car and cried for at least 30 minutes. So many emotions were running through my mind. I kept saying he hit me, over and over repeatedly. I was in shock. But the worst part was that my dad didn't respond like I thought he should have. It reminded me of that lady I saw helpless, scared, and running for help.

I had to get revenge. I couldn't just let Mike think he could get away with putting his hands on me! But how? After a few more minutes I got angry and knew what I had to do and who I needed to call!

RING RING RING

RING RING RING

"Pick up the phone!" I said.

RING RING RING

"Yo what up?" he answered.

I just began crying the minute I heard his voice.

"What's the matter?" he asked.

"Mike hit me!" I said with tears rolling down my face. "He punched me in the back of my head for something stupid. I'm tired and I can't take it anymore." I said.

"Roz, I know you not telling me this nigga put his hands on you. I told that fool he better treat your right!" he said sounding pissed.

"Where are you", he asked.

"I'm on Lance Street by the train tracks" I said.

"Ok, stay in yo car. I'm on my way." he said.

"Thank you Derrick." I answered.

It wasn't long before he rolled up and told me to get in his car.

"Roz, where is he now?" he asked.

"I'm not sure probably at the house." I said.

When I got in the car, I already knew what was going to be on the inside. Derrick had his gun sitting right on his lap. He was hard core. He wasn't the type to reason with and talk things over.

We pulled up to the house and it was pitch black dark.

"He must be gone." I said.

"He ain't got no car and the nigga never had money. So, he couldn't have gone far." He said.

"You get out and go knock on the door." He said. "Don't worry, I'm going to handle it. You just get him to open the door." Derrick said in a very serious and low tone.

I got out of the car and walked up the steps so scared. I knew what was about to happen. Mike was about to get the payback of his life. I was so angry and hurt that I didn't care anymore.

KNOCK, KNOCK, KNOCK

"Mike?" I said. "It's Roz."

KNOCK, KNOCK, KNOCK

"Mike...open the door!" I yelled.

BANG, BANG, BANG

There was no motion going on at all in the house. Suddenly, I heard a door open. He lived in a double, and the neighbor Jerry poked his head outside.

"Hey Hun, what's going on?" Jerry politely asked.

"I'm looking for Mike. He was just here a while ago. We had a real bad argument." "Have you seen him?" I asked.

"No baby girl." he said. "I haven't seen him."

"Ok", I replied.

I walked away wondering if Jerry was telling the truth. He didn't miss a thing. I would not have been surprised if Mike was hiding out inside his house. It was pitch black dark, so I couldn't see anything. I know now it was for the best.

I got back in the car and just began to cry.

"Where ya boy at?" asked Big Boy.

"I guess he left, so we can go." I said.

"You want me to go get a hotel and you can chill there for tonight?" Derrick asked.

"I'm tired," I said.

"Ok, I'll get the hotel room," replied Derrick.

"No, not sleepy, tired. I'm tired, done, ready to go back home."

I was ready to go back home. I knew it was over between Mike and me. There was no way I about to give Derrick the impression anything would be happening between us. I was tired of being used and abused and ready to go home. I would have to just face whatever consequences lies ahead. I no longer had a key so, I was forced to make that phone call.

RING, RING, RING......

52191

After I stopped seeing Mike, it was difficult, but I had no choice but to move back home. The very place I was running to get away from was the very place I was now running to get back to. My parents never said much about Mike nor about my partying and drinking, well at least my dad never mentioned anything. My mom on the other hand took a shot at me most times she had the opportunity. It was expected. It was also a constant reminder that I had messed up.

Amid all my mess, I managed to keep my job on campus working as a server for the school catering company. It was a nice job. We would deliver refreshments and meals for all the meetings on campus. Even the parties hosted at the Chancellor's house. Great job, great co-workers, but not great money.

My co-worker, Dawn who had been working there for a while, felt the same way. So, we made it a point to begin an intense job search. We checked the papers, local listings, and for any kind of job lead, we were on it.

One day Dawn had an interview downtown in between classes at a very nice hotel. She needed to get there and back by a certain time, so I was able to help her out with transportation. It wasn't much but I still had two-toned Bertha. We made it there on time and because I didn't want to pay for parking, I decided to circle the block until Dawn was ready. It was the longest hour. I kept circling and circling and circling. A few times, I parked illegally until I saw the meter maid turn the corner. Anyway, she was finally done. After circling back to the entrance, Dawn jumped in and we were headed back to campus.

"So how did it go," I said.

"Roz it went really well!", exclaimed Dawn. "I should hear something soon."

A few days went by and I was back to the routine of going to class, work, home, and then studying. The next morning, repeat and add typing a paper or two.

Once evening I got the craziest phone call…

　　　"Hello?" I asked.

This was before cell phones and caller ID.

　　　"Hey girl, it's Dawn." She replied. "Guess what?" she asked. "The hotel called and offered me the job." she explained. Dawn was searching for a better job for a long time, but she didn't sound excited at all. She almost sound depressed.

　　　"That's great!" I screamed. "When do you start?" I asked.

"I'm not," she replied. "The hours are flex, some 6a-3p and some 3p-11p. Without a car, I really can't commit to that on a bus. That why I recommended you for the position!"

"WAIT.... uh....what?" I was confused. "Dawn what are you talking about?"

"I told the lady in HR that I have a friend who is a hard worker with a good personality and transportation that would be great for the job!" she explained. "Her name is Claire and all you need to do is call her tomorrow if you are interested."

"Dawn, I can't take your job!" I said. "You have been wanting something better and this is it!" I explained.

"Roz, it's ok." Dawn said in an assuring voice. "I want you to call."

"Ok, thank you so much Dawn." I said. "What's the number? I'll call tomorrow."

The next day, I got through with my morning classes and decided to call about the job.

I called and spoke to Claire in Human Resources, and it was true. She interviewed Dawn and offered her the job but because she didn't have adequate transportation, she told the manager about me. I never applied to this company, but before I got off the phone, I had an interview set up for the next day at 10am.

The next morning, I was up preparing what I was going to say and how to say it. I was practicing my firm hand shake and eye to eye contact. It was a great opportunity for me to make more money. The good thing is that I knew exactly where to go. The bad thing is that I had to pay to park. I finally made it to my destination and walked in the Human Resources office looking and feeling good. "Good Morning, my name is Rosalind Armstrong." I have a 10 o'clock appointment with Ms. Claire."

There were several people in the office I assume waiting for their chance to shine also.

"Ms. Rosalind Armstrong? Hi I'm Claire." she said.

The initial interview went very well. I was nervous but at the same time thinking something good has got to happen because it's wild how I even got this interview. Well, not only did I have an initial interview, it was a 2-week process of interviews. I spoke with the HR manager and the Department manager. I even interviewed with the General Manager. This was a 5 Star hotel and they were very selective about their new hires that would have direct contact with the guests. After ALL the interviews, I was offered a FT evening/weekend position, which I gladly accepted!!

"Dawn, guess what?" I said

"Ummm, let's see…you got the job!" Dawn shouted with great anticipation in her voice.

I screamed, "I GOT THE JOB!! Thank you so much for even mentioning my name. It's like a dream, really! I have a job with great benefits!!!"

"You're welcome and you deserve it Roz. So, when do you start?" Dawn asked.

"May 21st," I replied.

I Surrender

The past few months had been difficult, but I felt like everything was finally turning around in my life. I was back on track with school, living at home, and focusing on me. I had been working at the hotel for a few weeks attending orientation meetings and trainings, so I hadn't met a lot of the employees yet. But I knew it would be a matter of time.

I stepped on the elevator this day, on my way to lunch and there was this guy standing to the corner of elevator, very quiet, but also very cute. I could tell he worked there because of the black and white uniform he was wearing. We had 11 floors to ride down, so I decided to introduce myself.

"Hello, I'm Rosalind!" I said very bubbly.

"Hi, I'm Dwayne," he replied in a very, very shy voice.

"I just started working in room service and am still trying to meet people." I explained. "Where do you work?" I asked.

"I work in Housekeeping." He said.

That was it.. He was so shy. It was obvious I was trying to start a conversation, but it was not going to happen if I waited on him.

"So, I'm new, like I said and just trying to meet people." I explained. "So far, I like the job!" rambling on and trying to get as much conversation in before we got to the basement.

"Do you like the job?" I asked

"Yes," he said.

By this time the elevator opened at the basement level and we both surprisingly started to walk in the same direction. I was headed to the cafeteria and he was going to the Housekeeping Department, which just so happened to be in the same way. I talked non-stop until we reached the office door.

"Ok Dwayne, nice meeting you. So, when you see me make sure you speak.", asking and suggesting at the same time.

He said ok and quickly went into the office as I continued walking towards the employee cafeteria. I wasn't sure if he was that nervous or if my talking scared him.

A couple of weeks went by and I ran into Dwayne again at work. This time he was a little more relaxed.

"Hey Dwayne, remember me?" I asked

"Yes, Rosalind, right?" he replied.

"That's right." I answered. "How have you been? I haven't seen you since we met a few weeks ago." I asked.

"I've been good. How are you?" He asked.

"I'm good still learning," I said.

Even though Dwayne was more relaxed he was still hesitant in his conversation.

"What time are you going to lunch today?" he asked.

"It all depends on how busy it is in room service. Why?" I asked.

"Well, I umm, I would like to just sit and talk. You know if you had time." He said very reluctantly.

"Ok, that sounds good." I said.

The next hour or so I was anticipating going to lunch to sit and talk. From what I could tell Dwayne was quiet, shy, and very nervous. He was also handsome and fine. I pray I wasn't smiling too hard or blushing at the fact that he wanted to go to lunch. The minute things slowed down in room service, I decided to head to lunch. He told me to stop in the housekeeping office and ask the receptionist to tell him I was downstairs. So, I did.

I decided to wait in the cafeteria and order my food. I didn't really know what to expect from our conversation. I also didn't want to be super excited, but I was so taken by his pretty brown eyes. I got my lunch tray and found a table. Waiting. A few minutes later, he walked in.

It was pretty obvious we were both looking for each other because we both made immediate eye contact the second, he walked in. We gave each other a warm smile. After he ordered his lunch he headed to the table.

"Hey, I was hoping you got the message." I said.

"Oh yeah, I told Ms. Mary you were going to leave me a message. It was no problem." he said.

We sat there talking and getting to know each other with the few minutes we had. Lunch was 30 minutes, but it takes 5 minutes to catch the elevator to the basement and another 5 minutes to order and wait for you food. So really you had a good 20 minutes. But we made the most of our time. The conversation was good mainly asking the standard questions: what school did you attend, where did you grow up?? These are standard questions for New Orleanians. Then I asked a question that was the highlight of lunch.

"So how long have you been working here?" I asked.

"Today makes 1 month." He replied.

"Really, I've been here exactly one month." I said. "That can't be right because I never saw you until two weeks ago. My hire date was May 21st. Show me your ID."

Dwayne reached into his wallet and shows me his employee ID with a hire date of May 21st. We were in the building together that same day and never saw each other until four weeks later.

The next few weeks, were filled with LOTS of getting-to-know-you lunches. He was nice. He was almost too nice. Unfortunately, I was used to the "bad boy" and he was a "momma's boy". Real soon after, I found myself not being interested in Dwayne anymore. He was just too, too nice. A day never went by without Dwayne bringing me flowers or candy. NEVER! Nobody ever did those type of things. He was very

197

giving while I was used to others taking. He would always come up to my department to say hello. When I would leave to go home, a note from him would be waiting for me on my car window, asking me to call him. This happened several nights. I politely threw the note away and thought to myself, stalker alert!

As the old folk would say, he was definitely "courting" me. But it was all too new and overwhelming to me. Even though I was back at home, I was still trying to go out with girlfriends and drink. The strip club was still calling me on the weekend and of course Friday was Ladies night! Dwayne was nice but.... I wasn't ready for any type of relationship. Then it happened...my car, two-toned Bertha, started giving me problems and soon went to car heaven. Well Dwayne saw this as his opportunity. I started taking the bus in the afternoon to get to work, but a female riding the bus at midnight to get home wasn't wise. I needed a ride home from work and guess who was always available. Dwayne would sometimes get off his shift at 8 or 9'o clock and wait...PATIENTLY... for my shift to end so he could bring me home. He never complained if I got delayed wrapping up paperwork. He never asked how long? He would sometimes STAND and read the newspaper right outside the department door, so I couldn't help but walk right into him when I left. Because of all the attention he was giving me, I started to hate it. I didn't want to have anything to do with Dwayne. Even though it was flattering, I just didn't want that attention. It began to bother me.

Obviously, there was an attraction that kept Dwayne in the picture. The one thing I did appreciate was his kindness. He was just a kind person and I liked that quality. I don't know if I felt sorry for him or what, but if nothing else, he deserved a call after all the money he spent in the vending machine buying me candy every day. So, I finally decided to give him a call and surprisingly, we had a great conversation. By the end of our first phone conversation, we had agreed to go out on a first date to the movies the following Friday night, because we were both off.

Since I was living back at home and had no transportation, he would come to pick me up from the house. Which meant he was going to meet my parents. Now my parents are, well my parents. I was a little nervous because my dad can seem intimidating, but he's the sweetest and most generous man I know. However, he's also able to go from 0 to 1000 in 0.3 seconds, if you press the right button. Last, but not least, he was also in a backslidden state at the time, so every other word he said was a cuss word. Seriously. My mom on the other hand, was notorious for asking 1000 questions. For EVERYTHING! But to make matters worse, once she asked the questions and got an answer, she would not understand the answer and repeat some of the questions repeatedly. Sure, come on over Dwayne, this will be fun.

"Hey Dwayne, come on in", I said.

My dad made the living room his sanctuary. After he came home from work and showered, he remained in the living room relaxing and watching his T.V. programs.

"Daddy this is Dwayne and Dwayne this is my dad." I said. They greeted each other with a firm hand shake and immediately started talking. Shortly after, my mom came into the living room. "Dwayne this is my mom. Momma this is Dwayne." I said.

"Hello Mrs. Armstrong, nice to meet you." He said

"Likewise." Momma said.

I went back upstairs for a few more minutes to finish getting ready while my dad and Dwayne talked. This was a totally different scenario from when Mike met my dad. After about 15 minutes, it was time to go. I came downstairs somewhat excited, somewhat nervous, and somewhat unsure. But I said I would go...so let's go.

"Ok, y'all we are about to go to the movies. I'll be back later." I said.

My dad was cool, but my mom had this crazy smirk on her face. A look I didn't want to entertain at all.

We headed for the movie and the conversation in the car was nice. Of course, we talked about the job and the interesting people we worked with every day. I couldn't wait to see the movie called In Living Color. I was told that it was good, so I knew that meant a lot of people would be at the theater and it might be crowded. We made it to the theater and purchased our tickets. There seemed to be a nice crowd that night. But we were set. We had our snacks and great seats. Now all we needed was for the movie to begin. Not many people were in the theater. In fact. Dwayne and I were the ONLY two people in the entire the theater. I thought it was some kind of joke, or, wondering if Dwayne had something to do with that. No one else was in the entire movie. It was just the two of us and we had a great time.

I honestly thought Dwayne had talked to the people and set that up. He was a "low key stalker." That was the one and only time I have ever experienced that. Needless to say, the rest of the night's conversation topic was set. We laughed and laughed. It also somewhat made me pull back for a brief moment and wonder how this happened. Why did this happen? Was this supposed to happen? The end of the night came quick after a nice ride home. We said goodnight and that was it, or so I supposed.

That night sparked a little more interest in Dwayne. This all started in May of 1991. Our first "date" to the movies was in August. Whenever we worked the same shift, we would take our lunch breaks together. He would give me a ride home, most nights. The candy and flowers kept appearing in my department. Because we worked in a hotel, there was always a banquet function taking place in the ballrooms. After the event was off, the staff would discard all the table trash, including the fresh flowers that were used as centerpieces. Well, Dwayne would time it just right and go to the ballroom to and remove all the flowers from the tables and make a bouquet for me! If Dwayne was off, he would send somebody to Room Service with flowers or candy or something special. Who does that?! He was super sweet and always there when I needed anything. Again, he was almost too sweet. I had never been treated with so much respect and thoughtfulness.

At this point, it was obvious we liked one another, but I was still hesitant. We did the group thing at night after work with other co-workers, shooting pool. I LOVE pool! I remember watching my dad play at my uncle's bar. In my opinion, my dad was the best pool player ever. He owned his personal set of pool sticks and I thought that was so cool. Anyway, I enjoyed hanging out with the group after work drinking and shooting pool. I extended the invite to Dwayne to hang out, so he did. I think Dwayne would have gone any place I suggested. And as always, he was kind and hung out as late I wanted to be out in order to drive me home. A little while later, we even shared our first kiss and it was very nice.

I don't even know when it officially happened, but maybe a month later, Dwayne and I were a couple. I guess, all the notes, candy, and flowers finally paid off. We started spending a lot of time with each other. I liked being with Dwayne because he made me feel safe. One of our favorite things to do was to get po-boys from Hank's with a Big Shot and go sit on the Lake. As often as we could, we had po-boy dates and I really loved them. We would talk about our families, which were quite different. Most times, we talked about work. A good bit of the time, our conversation was about school. I was pressing to get through and get out of college. So this went on for a while. Going to the lake. Shooting pool after work. Unfortunately, there was one major problem. I was beginning to develop feelings for Dwayne. But the feelings wasn't the problem. It was My Past! I had never shared with Dwayne about all the men I dealt with in the past. And I definitely didn't tell him about all the STDs. I KNEW that would be a "deal breaker." It was an ugly past that I wanted to erase and never let reappear.

One conclusion I made up in my mind was the strong possibility of being single for the rest of my life. Who in the world would ever want to be with someone so used, someone so scarred, someone who, in my opinion, was dirty. I was determined to keep this a secret until the grave. The likelihood of having a husband, let alone a family was now a fantasy. In my multiple trips of going back and forth to the doctor, taking medication, one of them said having children would be a risk, if I was able to have children at all. So, this would probably be a temporary "thing" with Dwayne. But what should have fizzled out continued to spark. The last two months we became inseparable (shout out to Natalie)!

Now it was December and it was getting close to the big company Christmas party, which was our official stepping out as a "couple." People knew Dwayne liked me and vice versa, but we always made sure to let everyone know it wasn't official, official. I love parties and dancing and this night was almost magical to me. He picked me up from the house, looking so so good and debonair! My mom even took picks of us, like it was prom. When we got to the party hand in hand it was like the entire company was excited for us. Ok, almost the entire company. There were beaucoup girls that wanted Dwayne. So not everyone celebrated...there were some haters. Sorry girls, he's with me.

What I loved about Dwayne, and still do, is that he treated me like a queen, with

RESPECT! He put me on a pedestal and whatever I want, he tries his very best to succeed at getting it. The rest of that evening we laughed and enjoyed one another.

So much had changed in just 6 months of my life. A new job and what seemed to be a new relationship. The end of the year was definitely better than the way it started off. I was still in the military and headed for a two week tour to Egypt on December 31st. While Dwayne and his family were headed to church to bring in the New Year, I was at the airport about to fly out. I remember calling Dwayne before we started to board to say Happy New Year and I love you.

Out with the old and in with the new. I was back in the states and once again kicking it with Dwayne. We got on the subject of church, again, and Dwayne would invite me to come. I really didn't want to have anything to do with "church". It was so boring. I couldn't understand what the Reverend was even talking about. That's why I wasn't in church at that point. I couldn't wait until I was old enough to make my own decisions and my mom didn't pressure me about it after I got back from basic training. Besides, I would be out late on Saturday and sometimes didn't come home purposely until Sunday night or a few days later. So sorry, looks like I missed church again.

It seemed like he was always asking me to go to church. LEAVE ME ALONE is what I wanted to say but never did. This went on for a while until I finally agreed to go. It was for Easter Sunday. I hadn't been to church in a minute and I was just so glad I survived finding a decent outfit. Now me agreeing to go with him and his family was a big deal, especially because of the church they attended. I heard so much about the Reverend. He was taking all the money. Also, if you were even thinking about becoming a member, you had to fill out an application and give them your W2 form. Yes, I heard all about it and I wasn't about to get suckered into it.

The service was held in the Arena. Are you kidding me? Who does that? We had to park and walk and finally got a seat, way up at the top. It was interesting. There were so many people singing and excited about everything. I was taking it all in...a little judgmental and suspicious at times. Well, he, the Reverend that takes all the money, finally came on the stage to give the sermon. He didn't ask for it but the person before him had already hit the people up. I was waiting to hear what he was about to say...was the topic going to be about money? But to my surprise he never ONCE said the word money. He never ONCE said anything about it. I can't remember the topic because it's been so long ago, but what I do remember quite well is that it was uplifting. It was Easter Sunday, so of course he talked about Jesus, but it was something different. I was so focused on every word he was saying. I never got distracted. But what blew me away is when he began to sing. Well he didn't sing, he SANG! It was amazing. I was in semi-shock that it was church, and I was somewhat enjoying it.

After he sang, he began to ask people to make a decision for Jesus Christ. We were sitting up high in the balcony, as well as others, but that didn't stop the droves of people, young and old walking all the way to the front of the stage. I had never seen anything like that before, ever. I watched in amazement. Suddenly, I had this weird feeling. It was as if I was getting nervous or anxious. Then I started to cry. Luckily, I was sitting on the far end of everyone. I just turned my head and wiped away my tears. Nobody noticed because I was too cool for that. I was confused. Why in the world am I crying? I was talking to myself saying, "Roz, get it together." Eventually, the people stopped coming. Everyone was excited for them, clapping and happy. After a few more formalities, everybody began to leave, and church was over. But little did I know it wasn't over for me. The rest of the day was strange. I was replaying the service over and over in my head. Trying to move on but couldn't.

The next week, I remember calling Dwayne asking what was going on at the church. He said bible study. Before I knew it, I asked to go. I was curious to see if that same feeling would happen again. Bible study was different. Not a lot of singing and dancing or shouting. I was trying to relax because I had never attended bible study in my life. Thinking back, it's kind of funny because I didn't know what was going on. I was curious. I enjoyed it. But that's crazy. Church is for old people. This is not for me. I kept having these conversations in my head about "church." I started going to a few Sunday morning services, and I enjoyed that too. It was strange. I can't do this. I can't do this. I was fighting something but didn't know what. It was a feeling because there was nothing physically there. Fighting emotions that this excitement was only temporary. So, my solution, leave this Jesus stuff alone.

Dwayne had gotten into a routine of asking me to church whenever I was off. But I made up in my mind that wasn't for me.

"Hey Roz", the voice on the other end of the phone said.

It was my dear friend, and club hopping ride or die, Terri. Terri and I go way back to 7th grade. She was always fun to be around especially in the club. We would do Ladies Night, Stripper Night and every other night! Well she was calling about Saturday night and I was ready. We went out and had a ball. The men were paying, and we were slaying. I danced, laughed and got ridiculously drunk. It must have been close to 3am when I got home, and I crashed. I jumped straight in the bed.

RING RING RING

"Hello," I said trying to get the frog out of my throat.

"It's Dwayne," he said. "I'll be there to get you around 10 o'clock for church.

Apparently, I told him I would go this Sunday, because he didn't ask. He was calling to give me a time. What's crazy is that I agreed to go, knowing I was messed up. I dragged myself out of the bed and somehow got it together in between the nausea and sweating. There was definitely a war going on that morning because my mind was telling me are you CRAZY! Call him back and tell him you're not going. You won't be going this Sunday or any other Sunday. But my body was doing something different. My motions were slow but still picking out clothes and getting dressed. It was horrible because I kept going to the bathroom and then I was sweating out all that alcohol. But I never called him back to say I changed my mind.

Dwayne finally arrived, and we headed to church. The sun was SO BRIGHT THIS DAY! I needed sunglasses to make it to the car. Then I started sweating again because of the alcohol and now the heat. I just kept thinking to myself, I just need to get through service, so I can come home and sleep the rest of this off. The church service was really all a blur to me. I can't remember what the preacher said or what inspiring songs were sung that day. I do remember having my shades on at one point, sweating, and going to the bathroom. I was there physically, but my mind was on my nice bed. Finally, the preacher stopped preaching and began to ask people to come to Jesus. I don't remember what the sermon was about. I don't remember any songs. But I do know something touched me THAT day. Amid the preacher asking people to come, I was sitting there once again, now sweating and anxious. It was as if I came alive to everything that was taking place. I went from sitting there half sleep and hungover to standing up from the middle section and making my way to the center aisle. I will never forget what happened next.

I had been promiscuous for years. Everything was about men, sex, drinking, and having a good time. As I walked up that center aisle, I could feel chains breaking and falling off my body!

It was liberating. It was refreshing. It was as if I stepped into an entire new world! Once I made it to the front, I just began to cry! I couldn't stop! I was also shaking like a leaf but not in a fearful way, but almost electrifying. I knew then that my life would NEVER be the same.

They escorted all of us that walked up to a smaller room to talk about what happens next. I was baptized when I was 10 years old, so I didn't think I could re-do that. I was what the "church" called a backslider. Once had a relationship with Christ and then as I like to say did the Michael Jackson "moonwalk" right out the back door. Everyone was so nice and just as excited as the people in the room.

When I left out of the room, Dwayne was there waiting with a huge smile on his face. I wanted to say why didn't you tell me I could be so free!!! But I guess all those invites to come to church was his way of saying you need to get it together…lol! I was feeling great and I could tell Dwayne was very happy for me as well. There was one small problem that I had to deal with, my parents! I had to tell Louis and Thelma that I'm back in church. But the church I have decided to join is the one both had issues with. You see most of the things I heard about this church and the Reverend came from home. But I needed to tell them, I am making a change.

Even though I don't know the last time I went to my "home" church, I still was a "member", I guess?? It was where my foundation began, where I was baptized, sang in the youth choir, attended vacation bible school, and stood once a month with a tissue bobby-pinned in my hair to tell the church my determination. My determination is to make heaven my home...then I sat down. I didn't fully know what or why I was saying it. When I would stand in Pilgrim Progress Missionary Baptist Church to say that, I wanted to go to heaven but determined? Hummmm, I didn't know what that meant. Anyway, I knew I needed to let them know I was back in church and that I was so excited. We drove back to Dwayne's house and I decided to call my parents, so he could share in the good news.

"Hey daddy, it's Cat!" I said with excitement in my voice.

"Hey Cat, how you are doing?" he asked.

"I'm doing good." I replied. "Guess what daddy?" I asked. Before he had an opportunity to speak, I immediately started explaining what happened today.

"I joined church today!" I said.

"You what, nah what you did, you joined church?" he asked.

"Yes!" I said. "I rededicated my life today and joined Greater! No more drinking or partying. I'm done!" I explained.

"Well Cat, I don't know about that." He said. "Let me put your momma on the phone. Hold on." He said.

It was very strange because there was no excitement in return. I was wondering what in the world was going on. In the background, I could hear my dad calling my mom to the phone in a hurry. "Thelma!" he shouted.

No reply from my mom.

"Oh Thelma!" daddy yelled. "Come to the phone and talk to your daughter." He said.

"Yeah, hello," she said.

"Hey Ma," I said. "Did daddy just tell you? I joined church today!" I asked.

I was waiting for the approval.

I was waiting on the support.

I was waiting on the encouragement.

Instead, it was just the complete opposite.

My mom said, "What do you mean you joined church today, where?"

I said, "I joined Greater Saint Stephens today! I'm not going out anymore. I'm not going to drink anymore. I'm so excited and I wanted to tell you and daddy."

My mom was not excited. In fact, she and my dad very upset that I had join THIS church. My dad was in the background saying all kind of stuff. They both asked if I had to give my W2 form to join. It was crazy! Both of my parents seemed disappointed. I really could not understand or believe what was happening.

"Roz, did you do this because of Dwayne?" she asked.

"What do you mean?" I said. "I did this today because of me! Nobody forced me to join church." I said very sternly.

I could feel myself about to explode. So, the call was officially over.

"Ok, well I was just calling thinking you all would be happy. I'll see y'all later." I said with disappointment.

I ended the call and I wanted to cry my eyes out. I was crushed because my parents were feeling some kind of way and it didn't make a bit of sense.

Dwayne was sitting right there next to me and somewhat heard the entire conversation. He could also see the disappointment on my face.

"Well, my parents don't seem too happy." I said. "They both think the church is after your money." I explained. I decided not to tell Dwayne what my mom said about me joining because of him. It just wasn't the right time.

The rest of the day was bittersweet. Sweet because, I was absolutely thrilled about joining church. I was still on cloud 9!! Bitter because, I really thought my parents would have been somewhat glad, happy or maybe relieved. I went from running the streets, dressed half-naked most of the time, to dressed in all black the rest of the time and staying out for days at a time wherever to NOW saying I'm in church and my life has changed. It was still hard for me to process AND even HARDER to begin to understand them. How can a person be so happy and sad at the same time?!

Well, Pilgrim Progress MBC, that was the summer of 1992 and I was now finally determined to go to Heaven. I attended bible study classes, Sunday services, and deliverance services; you name it, I was there. I was so needing to know and understand more.

Dwayne and I continued to see each other and amid us learning about each other, Dwayne NEVER tried to take advantage of me. He was always a gentleman and a gentle-man! The time was now for me to "come clean" with Dwayne. I cared about him and my feelings were getting stronger and it was obvious that it was mutual. There was no way in the world I could NOT tell him about my past, we somehow really committed to one another, and he NOT know the issues I still deal with every day.

I had to do it. This was the day that I tell Dwayne EVERYTHING. He was scheduled to work 3-11, but I was off this day. I had made it up in my mind…just do it so we all can move on. On days we worked different schedules, he would let me keep the car. By this time, he purchased his own car and it was a great help that I was able to get off the RTA, so I was able to go with him to work and I'd keep the car until I'd have to pick him up. When I think back now… that day was the beginning of the cleansing.

"Dwayne, before you go into work, I need to talk to you about something." I said.

By this time, we made it to the hotel and parked. He looked at me as to say ok, what do you want to talk about?

"Ok, do you want to talk now?" he asked.

"Yes." I said.

I started the conversation, with what most people would say is a break-up line.

"You know I like you a lot, but…" I said.

Dwayne just sat there with this curious look on his face.

213

"What I'm about to say is very hard." I explained.

"Dwayne...." I said.

"Hummmm......well......you see...." I attempted to say.

When we parked there was a slight drizzle of rain and by the time, I finally got a few words out, it was pouring.

> "I just don't know how to tell you this." I said

> "Roz, it's ok just say it." He said.

I tried, and I tried and I tried, BUT I was so afraid to tell him. I was so scared to tell him.

There was a least 10 – 15 minutes of silence of me just sitting there struggling to talk. The one with a big mouth, a loud mouth, I couldn't speak. It was like I was choking on my own words. All you could hear was the rhythm of the hard rain drops beating on the window shield as we both sat there staring down.

Dwayne was so patient. He never rushed me. He never got frustrated. He never looked at his watch to see how late he was for work. He realized what I had to say was difficult and Dwayne allowed me to take all the time I needed.

"Dwayne, I really like you a lot. We've been having a good time together. You're kind, thoughtful, helpful, and sweet. You make me laugh. Oh, my goodness, very patient. Really you're what I need." I explained.

I could barely look at Dwayne because I was so ashamed. I looked down the entire time.

"I really like you a lot too Roz." He responded.

"That's the problem Dwayne. I like you too much and I sense this could get serious." I said.

"Yes, you're correct. I'm ready to be totally committed to you." He said.

"But Dwayne, what I'm trying to say is that I'm not this innocent girl. I have had some experiences with guys." I said.

"Roz, I'm not worried about 1 or 2 guys," he said.

"I was with several guys and had bad experiences. Dwayne, I slept around a lot and was foolish, careless and I contracted several STDs, 5 of them" I explained.

"I've been dealing with this in secret for about 1 ½ years now. I'm on constant medication and have routine doctors' visits. Two of the diseases are incurable. I will be dealing with this for the rest of my life. I can't have anyone in my life on an intimate level because I would put them at risk. Not a serious committed relationship that involves marriage and having kids. So, I had to tell you. I'm not clean. I feel dirty all the time. I know things are getting serious between us and I had to come clean as best as I could to tell you the truth. What would that be like because I desire to be with you for the long haul and a few years later I share with you about my past. I feel you deserve to know."

By this time, I was holding back the tears. I struggled at first to even talk, but by the time I got started I was pouring everything out!

Dwayne sat there quiet for a while. I just sat there staring at the rain.

"I'm sorry and I understand if you don't have anything to say. I get it." I said.

"Ummm Roz, I wasn't expecting you to say all of that. That was a lot." He said.

Again, total silence between us.

"What do you want to do?" I asked.

"I need some time to think about this. I really don't know right now." He said.

It was only fair. I understood, and I didn't give him a timeline on when to let me know. He got out of the car and I headed home. Around 10:45p, I headed back to the hotel to pick him up from work. It was kind of awkward when he got in the car. We talked, but it was like an elephant was riding in that small burgundy Hyundai with us.

He dropped me off at home and said goodnight. I felt all sorts of emotions running through me. Sadness, Disgust, Anger, Fear, Doubt, Pity, Rejection and Loneliness. I was on an emotional roller coaster.

A day passed, and I didn't hear from Dwayne. Another day passed and still nothing. I was also off from work, so I didn't get an opportunity to see him. It was probably best. Now I needed to prepare myself to move on.

Three days later....

RING, RING, RING

"Hello?" I said.

"Hey it's me." Said the voice on the other end of the phone.

"Hey, how are you? Are you ok?" I asked.

I'm ok. I'm going to come over if it's ok. I need to talk to you." He said.

"Yeah. Ok, I'll be here." I said.

I didn't know what to think at the end of the call. Dwayne sounded like he was ok. But I wasn't sure why he wanted to come over to talk. After two days of no communication, it was pretty obvious about his decision.

I just waited patiently and told myself not to cry no matter what. About 45 minutes later, Dwayne pulled up at my house. Because I just wanted to get this over with, I opened the door and walked outside before he had a chance to walk up and ring the doorbell. He got out of the car and walked towards the house.

"Hey." He said.

"Hey." I responded. "That was fast. I wasn't expecting you to come right over." I said.

I know I haven't called in a few days, but I didn't want our first time since the other day to be over the phone." He said. "Can we sit in the car and talk?"

Ok, that's fine." I said a little reluctantly.

We walked over to his car, and as always, he opened my car door, so I could get in. The first few moments were just weird.

"Are you ok?" I asked.

"Yes." He said. "I just thought it would be better if we talked face to face."

"Alright." I responded.

"I did a lot of thinking about our conversation the other day." He said. "I was shocked to hear about your past, the other men, and the STDs." "I know we have gotten close these last few months and I was hoping we could be more committed and have a serious relationship." He explained. "But I wasn't sure if I wanted to deal with your past."

"I like you a lot Roz." He said.

"I like too Dwayne." I responded. "So, what are you saying." I asked.

"I'm saying, I took these two days to think and pray about us." He explained. "Roz, I want to be with you. I have very strong feelings for you and I truly believe that you are the one."

"I don't want you to feel sorry for me." I said.

"Roz, I love you." He genuinely said.

"I love you too." I replied. "But I don't want to expose you to anything.

"I thought about everything. I will be fine. We will be fine." He said.

"I'm not turning back. I'm ready." I said.

"Neither me." He said.

By February 1993, we were engaged and by August, that same year, we were saying I Do. I was running after something that had changed my life. I was compelled and went for it with all my heart.

Religion or Relationship

Life had changed so much! Now married and busy in the church…. simply amazing! Despite the new beginning I was still having health challenges. I was back and forth to the doctor, constantly having outbreaks, and always on medication. I tried to cope as much as I could. Many days I couldn't even sit down because the pain was too unbearable. This is how things were. I didn't know any other way. I was always apologizing to my husband because my challenge interfered so much with our intimate life. I cried. I was upset at myself for the stupid decisions I made in the past. I was so stressed because I really thought this would ruin my marriage.

This night, I didn't know my life was about to change forever. There was a big women's conference being held at our "mother" church. Several ladies from our ministry, including me, registered to go. Still new to this "church" thing but I did have a desire to attend. It was so refreshing to learn about God's word. It was so refreshing to be amid women who worshipped. Well after all the accolades and announcements and other protocol stuff....it was finally time for the guest speaker to "speak." I had no idea what I was in store for. This lady by the name of Jackie McCollough literally spoke to my soul. She had such a raspy voice but full of power. She was so articulate and so passionate about God's word. I had never experienced anything like it before.

She had us turn our bibles to the story about a woman who had an issue of blood for 12 long years. WOAH!! I had never heard that story before. She explained how this woman became an outcast amongst the people. All the shame and humiliation she experienced. She told us how she went back and forth to the doctors spending everything she had and still no cure. Wait, WOAH!! She not only told us, but I saw it for myself right in the bible! This powerful woman of God explained to us how God can heal and wanted to heal us. WOAH, wait a minute! Healing?? What was that?? Healing, you mean not taking a pill, not going to the doctor every month, you mean a normal life?! Healing! I want it! I must have it! This woman in the bible went from incurable disease to healed in an instant when she believed and then acted on what she believed. She touched Jesus! She touched the hem of His garment and healing was manifested! My God! It was as if this power house was speaking directly to me. Nobody knew my issue other than my husband. I was way too embarrassed to tell anybody. I knew people would never understand. I was in so much bondage.... physically, mentally, emotionally, financially, and especially spiritually! But here it was, Jesus was saying I too can be healed! I had an encounter with the Lord that night that set me free! I received the Word and believed just like the woman in the bible that I was healed.

Not too long after the conference, I experienced another outbreak and was back at the doctor. I knew right then and there, I had a choice to make. I could choose to believe what I was experiencing was going to continue being my way of life or I could choose to believe and hold on to the Word of God. I believed that I was healed, and nothing was going to change my mind!

I continued taking medicine and continued having outbreaks but that didn't change what I believed in my heart! While taking the pills, I was constantly saying by Jesus' stripes I am healed. It was years from my diagnosis in 1989, to my encounter with the Word in 1996 until after 2001 things began to manifest! It was less and less trips to the doctor. It was less and less taking the medicine. It was as if I had to get so full of the Word that it had to consume me and consume the challenge in my body. Don't misunderstand. I believed that I was healed at the W.O.E. conference that night. It was settled in my heart. God didn't lie. I continued to trust Him, and, in his timing, manifestation happened.

Finding TRUE Love

"I love you."

Three words that I longed to hear all my life, but I really didn't know what "true love" even meant.

I was so used to thinking love was about emotions or this warm fuzzy feeling. But later in life, I discovered that love had very little to do with emotions and all about actions.

"I love you."

Do you even know what you are saying? I'm damaged goods. I'm used.

I thought love was based on doing the right things. If I'm good, then somebody will love you.

"I love you."

Ok let me make sure that I look presentable and appealing to the eye at all times. Surely, it will make someone love me.

"I love you."

Don't ever mess up or do the wrong thing because the minute, no the second you do, it's over!

"I love you."

It looks like nothing I would have ever thought it would look like. Nor was it any place I had looked. It wasn't the white picket fence or the knight in shining armor. It wasn't in the club. It was amazing. It was an old rugged cross!

He said, "I love you my daughter."

"I finally know because you gave your Son just for me" I said. "That's love."

"That's True Love my child. Unconditional. Forgiving. Non-condemning. Unselfish. Accepting. Everlasting Love!" God said.

I replied, "I'm so glad you found me," "I believe you and love you too."

Go Tell It, I Surrender ALL

We are looking for people with a testimony for our upcoming lock-in. This is what the announcement read. I kept thinking to myself, I have a testimony. The Lord did something in my life and I wanted to tell on God. Yup, I think that's a testimony. I'll go tell the elder, so she could put me on the list.

We were at Wednesday night bible study and I met with the elder after service. I was so nervous, but I felt this strong conviction to go ahead with this. I began to talk about my life, my past, and consequences I had experienced. I talked about the encounter I had with the Word and how God used Dwayne, a pure individual, to invite me to church. I didn't get a chance to finish before she threw her hand up, as if she was giving me a "brick wall" or "talk to the hand"

"I don't need to hear anymore." She said.

I was so embarrassed, I just slouched down on the bench. But when I looked back up, she was smiling.

"God is good. You can tell the rest Friday night at the lock in. You do have a testimony." "You ok?", She asked.

"Yes, I'm ok." I said.

Friday night was here and soon it would be time for me to tell MY testimony. But suddenly it was like I was having a panic attack. I became so fearful. Was I crazy?! What was I thinking?! I can't tell "these" people about my past!! This was a mistake!! But they had already announced that I would be coming forth with a testimony! OMG!!!

I was shaking like a leaf and the only thing on my mind was finding the nearest, quickest, exit!!! I literally was up NEXT after they finished singing a song. I remember bending down on the pew and looking to see how I could discreetly excuse myself, but it was possible.

We had the old "bench like" pews with the compartment to hold your bible on the back of each pew. There was a bible in front of me. I picked it up and kept thinking Lord help me! I can't do this. They will laugh and talk about me!

I opened the bible and could not even believe what I was reading. I knew God was real but, this moment, I didn't have one ounce of doubt that he was real and heard my cry! The bible fell open to a scripture that has set me free. It said:

Romans 8:1, There is therefore now NO condemnation to them which are in Christ Jesus, who walk not after the flesh, but after the Spirit.

At that moment, it was as if something lifted from my shoulders. I wasn't heavy. I was still nervous but not scared. I felt like I had this burst of strength to be bold. I felt the burden of condemnation was lifted from me. It was time. No longer could I keep it to myself. I later came across a scripture that says, where the Spirit of the Lord is there is liberty. And, We overcome by the blood of the Lamb and the Word of our Testimony.

When I finished giving my testimony, something erupted in the building. Women were screaming, some were crying, a few were just shouting because they too were set free. I told the whole story…the good, the bad, and the ugly. My life was on display that night. Not by accident, but by divine order. It was orchestrated and I participated.

Many women came up to me thanking me for giving the testimony. But what surprised me was that, a few even said it was similar to their story. They had never been able to share or tell anyone. Now here they were confiding in me. Telling me how I helped them. What! I helped you because I choose to tell my story! God you are amazing. The more I was able to talk and share with the women, the freer I felt. It wasn't the end, but just the beginning of what God was about to do in my life. It all changed when I let go of my insecurities, my doubt, my fear, my shame, my embarrassment, and my guilt.

I had to stop condemning myself because God NEVER held my past against me. In fact, God LOVED me so much that he chose me in my mess! He LOVED me so much, that he sent his son Jesus to die for me! I heard a wise Pastor say, there is nothing you can do to make God love you more. So, I never had to be perfect. It's impossible no matter how hard anyone would try. But this wise Pastor also said, there is also nothing you can do to make God love you any less! With ALL my mess ups, short comings, mistakes, failures, men, partying, drinking, promiscuity, and so on, GOD LOVED ME THE SAME! The only thing God can do is Love, because that's his very nature and essence!

I'm here today because of God's Mercy and God's Grace. Mercy is not giving a person what they deserved when they are wrong. Grace is giving a person what they don't deserve when you know they are wrong. Grace is extending kindness and thoughtfulness to the unworthy. It's God blessing us, even though we don't deserve it.

Everything I did was deserving of a penalty. I deserve to be sick with disease in my body. I deserve to be alone. I deserve to not be loved. Everything I did, I was wrong but His love covered me. I am where I am today as Mrs. Dwayne C. Woodfox Sr. because of God's Grace! Someone who accepted me with all my flaws. A man pure in heart and body. I am where I am today as a mother of 4 gifted, talented and healthy children because of God's Grace! I am where I am today as a grateful grandmother to my very special & precious God-sent grandson because of God's Grace! I am where I am today as a Preacher of the Gospel because of God's Grace! I am where I am today as a published author, mentor, counselor, intercessor, and leader because of God's Grace! I didn't and still don't deserve these blessings, but God is Faithful. God is Forgiving, and God is Good!

I just needed to let go and trust God because his thoughts and plans toward me are thoughts of peace and not of evil. Thoughts to give me a future and a hope!

"Yes Lord, I Surrender ALL!" I said. And my life has never been the same.

This is my Story. My Testimony. My Deliverance

Prayer of Salvation

If you're holding this book, it was not by accident. It was written with you in mind. After reading this book, you realize you're not in right standing with God. You have never truly repented and you have never prayed the Sinner's pray or accepted him into your heart. The bible says in Romans 3:23, for all have sinned and come short of the Glory of God. That's what happened to me. I was deep in sin and I was enjoying the sin. But then life happened and things weren't much fun anymore. It was my choice, but to every choice there is a consequence. Because I was choosing at the time to live in sin, I was going to pay the price. You see, "the wages of sin is death, but the gift of God is eternal life through Christ Jesus says Romans 6:23.

While I was drinking, sleeping around, partying, and destroying my future, God loved me so much and put a plan in place to save me. Romans 5:8 say, while we were yet sinners

Christ died for the ungodly. I was the ungodly. It was because of his love, I'm here today. I invite you to join the Family of God! Accept Christ right NOW THIS moment! I make a bold statement when I say this, but Your Life will NEVER be the same!

Say this Prayer of Repentance out loud:

Dear Lord God, forgive me of my sins. I fell and came short of your glory. I was wrong. I was disobedient. I messed up and now I'm asking you to forgive me. Come into my heart and clean up the mess. Create in me a clean heart and renew the right Spirit within in. I'll serve you the rest of my days and I believe that Jesus is Lord that he died for my sins that he rose for my victory. I claim that victory and I believe that I am Saved, I am delivered, and I am Set-Free, In Jesus Name! Amen!

If you prayed that prayer, I want to celebrate with you! Please contact me at: reachingsisters@gmail.com

Welcome to the Family of God!

Nuggets

It was important that I continued to fill my heart, my mind, and my spirit with the Word of God, as it relates to healing. I suffered many, many years because I was ignorant to what the Word of God said about healing, both physical and emotional healing. If you are dealing with a Physical or Emotional challenge, I encourage you, I challenge you, to follow this daily prescription. No, I am not a doctor, nor claim to be one. But I am a believer that the Word works because in the beginning was the Word and the Word was with God and the Word was God. The same was in the beginning with God and all things were made by the Word and without the Word was not anything made that was made (John 1:1-3). You have to WORK THE WORD!

(1) Find a specific scripture about your situation. Read the scripture out loud once.

(2) Next read the scripture out loud again, but this time adding your name. Make the Word of God personal.

(3) Meditate, think, rehearse what that scripture looks like in your mind. Your mind is like a canvas. The Word of God will give you a Vision of your Future! Hide it in your heart and believe it is possible!

(4) Read the scripture out loud again, adding your name. Then say Thank You out loud, because what you just confessed with your mouth and believed in your heart, is already done!

(5) Repeat Steps 1 – 4, at a minimum 3x a day, 21 days STRAIGHT!!

Healing Meditation Scriptures

Psalms 34:19

Many are the afflictions of the righteous,

But the LORD delivers him out of them all. (NKVJ)

Psalms 103:1-5

Bless the LORD, O my soul; And all that is within me, bless His holy name!

2 Bless the LORD, O my soul, And forget not all His benefits:

3 Who forgives all your iniquities, Who heals all your diseases,

4 Who redeems your life from destruction, Who crowns you with lovingkindness and tender mercies,

5 Who satisfies your mouth with good things, So that your youth is renewed like the eagle's. (NKJV)

Psalms 107:1-2 Oh give thanks unto the Lord for He is good and His mercy endures forever. Let the redeemed of the Lord say so, who has redeemed us from the hand of the enemy. (KJV)

Psalms 107:20 He sent His word and healed them, and rescued them from their destruction. (Amplified Version)

Isaiah 53:5 But he was being punished for what we did. He was crushed because of our guilt. He took the punishment we deserved, and this brought us peace. We were healed because of his pain. (ERV)

Jeremiah 31:3

The LORD has appeared of old to me, saying:

"Yes, I have loved you with an everlasting love;

Therefore with lovingkindness I have drawn you. (NKJV)

Romans 8:1 There is therefore now no condemnation to them that are in Christ Jesus, who walk not after the flesh, but after the Spirit (KJV)

1 Pet. 2:24 Who Himself bore our sins in His own body on the tree, that we, having died to sins, might live for righteousness—by whose stripes you were healed. (NKJV)

Phil 4:6

6 Do not be anxious or worried about anything, but in everything [every circumstance and situation] by prayer and petition with thanksgiving, continue to make your [specific] requests known to God. 7 And the peace of God [that peace which reassures the heart, that peace] which transcends all understanding, [that peace which] stands guard over your hearts and your minds in Christ Jesus [is yours]. (Amplified Version)

Now add Your Story, Your Testimony, and Your Deliverance

_____

_____

_____

_____

_____

_____

_____

_____

_____

_____

_____

_____

_____

_____

_____

_____

_____

_____

_____

_____

_____

_____

_____

_____

_____

_____

_____

Meet the Author:

Rosalind Armstrong-Woodfox

Born and raised in New Orleans, LA. Rosalind Armstrong-Woodfox, is one of four siblings. She has been blessed in marriage to Dwayne for 25 years. She is also the proud mother of 4 and proud grandmother of 1.

Rosalind is a graduate of the University of New Orleans, where she earned a bachelor's degree in Political Science. She also served 8 years in the United States Army Reserve.

Rosalind is a founding member of Household of Faith Family Worship Church International, where Pastor Antoine M. Barriere is the Pastor and her Spiritual Father. She serves faithfully on the Elders Council and the church Trustee Board. She also serves as the Overseer of the Ministerial Alliance Ministry and is active in the Sisters by Faith Women's Ministry under the leadership of her 1st Lady, Dale Barriere. Rosalind is a servant, a mentor, a counselor, a worshipper, an exhorter, and a prayer warrior. You will always find her serving and meeting the needs of God's people and getting her "praise on!" Her daily motivation, Jeremiah 29:11, "For I know the thoughts that I think toward you, saith the Lord, thoughts of peace and not evil but to give you an expected end."

She loves to read, dance, bake, and trying new recipes. She's crazy about candles.... Yankee!! Also, bracelets & charm bracelets (which she wears every day). Not a big fan, but exercising is a part of her weekly routine. Nothing beats spending quality time with her family, especially her husband. But most of all, she loves spending time in God's word and preaching God's Word.

For speaking engagements send email request to:
Reachingsisters@gmail.com

Made in the USA
Columbia, SC
28 May 2019